KV-637-700

The Cross against the Bomb

BELL BAXTER HIGH SCHOOL
WESTFIELD RD.

THE CROSS
AGAINST
THE BOMB

Robin Gill

EPWORTH PRESS

© Robin Gill 1984

All rights reserved. No part of this
publication may be reproduced, stored
in a retrieval system, or transmitted,
in any form or by any means, electronic,
mechanical, photocopying, recording or
otherwise, without the prior permission
of the publisher, Epworth Press.

Gill, Robin
  The cross against the bomb.
  1. Atomic warfare——Religious aspects——
  Christianity
  I. Title
  261.8'73   BR115.A8

  ISBN 0-7162-0403-7

7162 0403 7

First published 1984
by Epworth Press
Room 195, 1 Central Buildings,
Westminster, London SW1

Printed in Great Britain by
Clifford Frost Ltd,
Wimbledon

Contents

Introduction

This book is written as a specific response to *The Cross and the Bomb,* edited by Dr Francis Bridger (Mowbrays 1983).[1] I believe that it is right occasionally for a book to be written as a specific response to another book – particularly if the issues are sufficiently important, the authors sufficiently noteworthy and their claims sufficiently contentious. In this case all three factors seem to be present. The nuclear issue could scarcely be more important, and might even be called *the* moral issue for our age. If we make the wrong decisions now there may be few moral decisions left to make, since there may be so few people left alive to make them. The nuclear debate is a debate not just about morality but about survival itself.

I believe that the views expressed in *The Cross and the Bomb* are sufficiently contentious to warrant a response. That book started as a response to the report of the working party under the chairmanship of the Bishop of Salisbury, *The Church and the Bomb* (Hodder & Stoughton 1982).[2] But it soon grew, 'from a particular reply to a particular report into a larger discussion of the moral case for multilateralism' (p. 1). Actually, it becomes evident that the book is now very much more than that. It seeks to justify nuclear deterrence on a moral and a Christian basis, to justify certain uses of nuclear weapons in terms of a traditional Christian just-war theory, and to show the irresponsibility of unilateralism and/or nuclear pacifism. The contributors are particularly offended that, in Christian circles especially, 'the unilateralist argument is frequently presented as morally self-evident' (p. 1). So, it is intended to be a polemical book and to contend what its authors believe to be wrong-headed beliefs within the churches. Because its contentions, if accepted by others within the churches, are so crucial and, in many respects, contrary to much of the present Christian ethos (as I shall argue in Chapter 6), they ought to be scrutinized carefully. It will be the aim of this book to attempt to do this.

I have attempted to set out the views of the various authors on specific issues carefully before criticizing them. And even then, I have tried to criticize views from within, without passing too many value-judgments about the authors themselves. But perhaps I can be allowed just one at the outset. I have found myself increasingly depressed by the low level of ethical and theological argument in so distinguished and influential a group of theologians. Only the article by the non-theologian, General Sir Hugh Beach, Warden of St George's House, Windsor Castle, makes a worthwhile contribution to the debate within the churches. It is for this reason that it forms the basis for Chapter 1 and plays a pivotal role in providing an empirical critique in the following chapters.

In attempting to scrutinize *The Cross and the Bomb* I have focused individual chapters on what I regard as its most contentious claims. Chapter 1, however, tries to set out some of the most important empirical facts about present-day nuclear weapons and deterrence. In common with the authors, I believe that it is vital that Christians who engage in the nuclear debate do so on the basis of a realistic and accurate assessment of the empirical situation. It serves no purpose to expound high-minded ideals which cannot be related to the crude political realities of the present-day world. The nuclear debate gets steadily more complex, and it is vital that, whilst not claiming to be an expert in strategy or defence issues, the theologian should make a serious attempt to become acquainted with the complexities. This chapter will also isolate those four contentions from *The Cross and the Bomb* which will be the subjects of the four chapters that follow. In the final chapter I will present my own understanding of the role of the Christian in a nuclear world.

If at times I appear to be excessively critical of some of the arguments used in *The Cross and the Bomb,* it is simply because these are crucial issues. This is not a game. Sometimes theologians are scorned for appearing to play with words, for wrapping up issues in needless jargon or for hiding behind recondite research. I do not share this scorn. Academic, detached research has yielded too many unexpected fruits in other disciplines for the theologian to be scorned in this way. None the less, I believe that the nuclear issue is too pressing for the moral arguments about it to be presented in too technical a manner. Without cluttering the text unnecessarily with footnotes, at crucial points I have attempted to indicate where the relevant critical research may be found. I believe that this is a debate which should engage all thinking people, and further I am convinced that it is a debate to which the Christian can make a special contribution. All thinking people should be concerned both about the survival of the world and about the means that their fellows adopt to ensure this survival. But, their belief in a God who created and redeemed this world gives Christians both additional reasons for these concerns and also a hope beyond them. Precisely because they believe that the world is 'given', the appropriate response for the creature to the Creator is gratitude and acceptance, not a determination to destroy the 'gift'. For Christians, the world is neither fortuitous nor sufficient in itself. It is a means, an essential means, to something else – to life with God. They cannot but be concerned if their neighbours appear determined to destroy this means or if those neighbours seem to be using immoral methods to avoid such destruction.

Finally, it is important to stress that these are issues which are enmeshed with ambiguities. If anyone claims to be certain that either unilateralism or multilateralism, nuclear pacifism or nuclear deterrence, is the *only* way to maintain the peace of the world, he or she is finding certainty where there can be none. The empirical and indeed moral consequences of nuclear weapons are still too new to the world for anyone to be certain. At times I will be critical of some of the contributors for reducing the issue of nuclear deterrence to the level of the playground analogy, when, in reality, the dimensions of nuclear weapons make such analogies ridiculously simplistic. There are no serious historical precedents for our present dilemma. Never before have we faced a situation in which a single terrorist group could destroy a whole city or in which the nuclear powers could destroy themselves and many others in minutes. The very lack of serious precedents makes moral conclusions so risky and yet so critical. Whoever does not feel these deep ambiguities, has not done justice to the nuclear issue. And whoever does not feel acute unease at the potential social consequences of any conclusions that they might reach is not acting with full moral responsibility.

I am most grateful to a number of people for helping me to prepare this book: to Professor Duncan Forrester of Edinburgh University and Dr John Elford of the Department of Social and Pastoral Theology, Manchester University, for reading an earlier draft; to my father, Dr Alan Gill, for correcting some of my bad English and bad logic; and to the Revd John Stacey and Epworth Press for producing this book so swiftly.

An attempt to do justice to crucial social and political issues is the central objective of the newly formed Centre for Theology and Public Issues at Edinburgh University. This unique resource, gathering together academics from a wide spectrum of interests and specialities, has encouraged me in the writing of this book and leads me to believe that the time is right for theologians to engage creatively, even if cautiously, with sympathetic non-theologians. There is a wider concern about moral and even specifically theological dimensions of social and political life than theologians themselves often recognize. This growing concern is evident *par excellence* in the nuclear debate. It is indeed a debate about survival itself and, as such, *should* be of central concern for theologians and for all those who will engage with them.

1 *Nuclear Weapons and Nuclear Deterrence*

It is important, at the outset, to distinguish between facts and theories in the nuclear debate. The existence of nuclear weapons, their potential destructiveness, their rapid expansion, their proliferation and their instability are all facts. Nuclear deterrence, on the other hand, is a theory. Despite the claims of some politicians, it is not a fact that nuclear weapons have prevented a European war since 1945. It is a theory which one may seek to justify or discount – a theory with few reliable precedents to act as guides.

Few would dispute the existence and potential destructiveness of nuclear weapons. The nuclear destruction of Hiroshima and Nagasaki was relatively minor compared with the potential destructiveness of modern nuclear weapons. The last forty years has seen a vast increase in human capacity for nuclear destruction.[3] Further, this potential destructiveness cannot be disinvented. It might be possible to destroy all existing nuclear weapons; it should be possible to reduce their number in the world; and, at some point, it must become essential to halt their accelerating increase. But the future potential for making nuclear weapons cannot be destroyed. Somehow the human race must continue to survive on this planet knowing that it always has the capacity to make nuclear weapons. Any realistic position in the nuclear debate must come to terms with this fact: mankind has the knowledge and capacity to make nuclear weapons (although, as I shall argue in the final chapter, this knowledge and capacity need not be used to make further, and still more destructive, nuclear weapons).

Again, it is a fact that nuclear weapons are expanding both vertically and horizontally. That is, they are becoming increasingly both more destructive and more a part of differing levels of strategic thinking. The vertical expansion of nuclear weapons should be obvious to all. It is common knowledge that both West and East now have the nuclear capacity to destroy humanity *in toto* and to leave behind an abundance of unused weapons. The world's nuclear armoury vastly exceeds its possible use. But what is also apparent is that within recent years nuclear weapons have also been expanding horizontally. If, at one time, the official Western nuclear policy was one of Mutually Assured Destruction (MAD), wherein the sole function of nuclear weapons was to deter the Soviet from a nuclear attack, by threatening their total destruction, today nuclear policy is far more complicated. Some nuclear weapons still have this function, but others are intended to have a much more specific strategic function (e.g. destroying weapon bases in the Soviet) and others still are intended for use against conventional forces. If once nuclear weapons were regarded as a final and suicidal resource, today they are regarded as an essential element of military defence at several levels. So, any serious and direct confrontation between West and East could result in nuclear warfare.

The extent to which nuclear weapons have expanded horizontally is made clear by Hugh Beach's careful and informed contribution to *The Cross and the Bomb*. In the British context, he distinguishes between the Polaris/Trident weapons which form Britain's independent nuclear forces (which he does not support) and the Tomahawk Cruise/Pershing II programme which forms the crucial part of NATO's nuclear forces (which he does support). Their total destructiveness is, of course, enormous. A single Polaris submarine alone carries 'more explosive power than all the munitions used in World War II put together' (p. 114). Tomahawk Cruise missiles and Pershing II missiles are quite different from each other. The first are 'low flying, air breathing missiles using a self-correcting internal guidance system and have much in common with unmanned aircraft, although only about twelve feet long. They each carry a single nuclear warhead but their ability to penetrate is high, since they fly below 250 feet directed by a guidance system whereby a computer compares the ground over which they are flying with a map stored in their memory. With a range of some 1,500 miles they have the capability to reach Moscow (just) but would take about three hours to do so. The launchers are highly mobile' (p. 120). Precisely because of their slow flight time and small numbers, Beach argues that they are 'utterly inappropriate for a disarming attack against the Soviet Union, let alone a "first strike". Consequently to categorize them as war-fighting weapons is incorrect: they are essentially weapons of deterrence' (p. 120). Pershing II, on the other hand, does have 'many of the characteristics of a first strike weapon', since it has 'a range in excess of 500 miles and [is] thus capable of striking targets [from Europe] well within the Soviet Union . . . Its time of flight is only fifteen minutes – consequently the Russians could have as little as ten minutes' warning or less. It is highly accurate and highly destructive' (p. 212). [4]

Interestingly, Beach argues that it is misleading to link NATO's Tomahawk Cruise/Pershing II programme with the deployment of Russian SS-20 missiles. It is not that the latter are any less destructive. They have a range of 3,000 miles and each can carry three warheads. But they are not a novel threat to the West: 'Since the early 1960s the Russians have had some 600 missile systems deployed in Russia, with ranges such that they can cover the whole of Europe but not the United States of America. The number of these missiles is being reduced as SS-20 is deployed and there is substance in the Soviet claim that this changeover represents no more than technical modernization of the system. [5] By contrast the Tomahawks and Pershing II are a threat to the Soviet homeland, from land based missiles in Europe, of a kind that has not existed before and must appear in Soviet eyes as an exact parallel, in terms of provocation, to the famous Soviet missiles in Cuba of the early 1960s' (pp. 121f.). Like Tomahawk Cruise missiles, the SS-20 missiles are mobile and thus present the West with no specific strategic target.

Finally, Beach discusses short range nuclear systems, which are not strategic, in the sense that they cannot reach Russia, but are rather intended for use against conventional forces:

'They exist in bewildering profusion. The most important functional distinction is that of range. *Shorter range* systems are those whose coverage (400-600 miles) is effectively of Eastern Europe, excluding Russia. Apart from the Pershing I ballistic missile . . . they consist entirely of aircraft, F-4, Jaguar, Buccaneer and Tornado, and F-104. *Short range* (or battlefield) systems consist of Lance ballistic missiles (range seventy miles) and eight inch and 155 mm Howitzers (range 15 miles). There are also nuclear warheads for Nike Hercules high level air defence missiles, and for land mines – known as Atomic Demolition Munitions (ADMs). The next most important distinction concerns ownership and control. The Jaguar, Buccaneer and Tornado aircraft are British owned and designed to carry free-fall nuclear bombs of British manufacture which remains at all times under British control. The remaining systems are all American, capable of carrying American nuclear warheads. All but the F4 and ADMs have been sold to allies: Pershing to the Federal German Republic (FRG); F-104 and Nike to the FRG, Belgium and the Netherlands; Lance and the Howitzers to those countries and the United Kingdom. But even so, the nuclear warheads remain at all times in American ownership and custody up to the moment of discharge. The number of these systems is also great. In NATO Europe there are some 500 such aircraft, 1,000 surface to surface missiles and Howitzers, and 6,000 nuclear warheads stored at fifty different sites (p. 124). [6]

It is with the short-range (rather than shorter-range) systems that the full extent of the horizontal nuclear expansion can be seen. Beach admits that, in military terms, their actual function is problematic: 'Ostensibly they exist to provide the necessary fire power to defeat a massive advance by forces of the Warsaw Pact. NATO doctrine specifically caters for what is ghoulishly known as nuclear "release" if conventional forces are in danger of being overrun and there is no other way of stopping the advance' (p. 125). But he does not believe that such an attack is likely, that such a defence will be effective or that it can avoid the danger of escalating such a war into a full-scale nuclear war.

Beach's account of present-day nuclear weaponry illustrates two more facts: nuclear weapons are proliferating and are becoming increasingly unstable. For all the talks on Strategic Arms Limitation (SALT) and Strategic Arms Reduction (START) and for all official policies of multilateralism, nuclear weapons are not only expanding but also proliferating. That is, there seems to be an ineluctable process according to which the number of countries possessing nuclear weapons grows from one decade to another. First it was the United States and Britain, then came Russia, and now we have France, South Africa, China, India . . . Countries such as Israel must have a nuclear capacity, and soon it may be parts of South America and North Africa.[7] At every point, policies of containment seem eventually to have failed, and few can be confident that some of the most politically volatile situations in the world will not soon be made more volatile by the presence of nuclear weapons. In the maze of shorter-range and short-range nuclear weapons that Beach describes, proliferation seems inevitable. With this proliferation goes an inherent instability. But even without proliferation the present nuclear situation is inherently unstable. The sheer volume of nuclear weapons possessed by NATO and the Soviet alone contributes to this instability, weapons produced beyond any conceivable capacity to deter. Even the technology supporting nuclear weapons provokes suspicions of instability. Until fifth-generation computers (i.e. computers which can give rational responses to enquiries) control the trigger and defence mechanisms of nuclear weapons, there will be serious doubts about stability and about whether either politicians or military are fully in control of existing weapons.[8] Finally, terrorism adds a horrific potential dimension to the nuclear debate. If a terrorist group comes to possess a nuclear weapon, it may be subject to none of the sanctions or precautions that may prevail in nuclear nations.

Not all experts would accept that 'instability' is an empirical fact about the present-day nuclear situation. The editor of *The Cross and the Bomb* includes, as an appendix, two talks by Michael Quinlan, who from 1977 to 1981 was Deputy Under-Secretary of State (Policy and Programmes) at the Ministry of Defence. He argues, forcefully, that there are a number of reasons for believing that the overall nuclear system is stable:

There is, for example, the very size of the armouries and the

knowledge of what they can do. No-one who lives with the facts
and has to think about them can ever be trigger-happy, or other
than enormously cautious . . . Five-figure numbers of these
awful weapons on each side are far too many, and I wish the
Russians had accepted the Carter proposals for deep cuts; but at
least these vast numbers do mean that no-one can suppose that he
could somehow ride the punch on tolerable terms. Next, despite
ups and downs, communication, understanding and agreement
between the two sides is far more extensive than it was, say, in the
1960s. The SALT I and SALT II agreements are in practice being
kept, even though the first has theoretically expired and the
second has not been ratified . . . There are practical agreements to
avoid conflict incidents, to explain accidents, to notify in
advance missile launch tests whose purpose might be
misunderstood, to consult together about dangerous
international situations. Intelligence, especially through satellite
photography, means that each side knows far more surely than
before what the other is doing. The delivery systems themselves
are far less vulnerable to preemptive strike than they used to be,
so there is far less incentive to launch first and ask questions
afterwards (p. 146).

The trouble is that this argument both ignores nuclear
proliferation and is itself a splendid argument for increased
proliferation. The whole is framed in terms of just two sides (NATO
and the Warsaw Pact) in the nuclear situation, which mutually
contain each other. It also suggests the conclusion that, if the
massive expansion of nuclear weapons has contributed to their
stability, then more countries should be encouraged to possess
them!

If all of these features of nuclear weapons – their existence,
destructiveness, expansion, proliferation and instability – seem to
be facts, their actual function is more debatable. Frequently in the
nuclear debate it is simply assumed without argument that
deterrence is the function of all nuclear weapons. There may be
some misgivings about whether or not this function is indefinitely
sustainable. There may be some disagreement about the social

grounds which require this function. There is often debate about the morality of nuclear deterrence. But it is frequently assumed to be a fact that the function of all nuclear weapons is to act as deterrents.

For much of his article Beach also seems to make this assumption. Yet there are occasional and highly significant admissions that deterrence cannot be the function of all nuclear weapons, as they exist at present. It has already been noted that he regards the status of short-range nuclear weapons as questionable in terms of their effectiveness as deterrents. He argues that 'nuclear strikes on the opposing front line are relatively ineffective. It is just here that troops are most widely dispersed and least vulnerable – either in slit trenches or under armour. Consequently the target list extends back to the second echelons; to concentration areas, bridges, air fields, marshalling yards, and control centres' (p. 126). As a result of this 'one should reckon, as the foreseeable consequence of such an exchange, a European death toll running once again into tens of millions, the overwhelming majority of whom would be civilian' (p. 127).

Again, Beach has problems in seeing the deterrent value of Britain's independent nuclear forces. He maintains, in his most striking argument, that 'no-one has yet succeeded (indeed there has [*sic*] been notably few attempts) to define circumstances in which it could conceivably make sense for the United Kingdom to use its Polaris/Trident force when the United States was unprepared to do so. Such use, by a country which presents an almost unique concentration of cities and industries, unprotected by any but the flimsiest of civil defence provision, against any potential assailant with nuclear weapons, would be blatantly suicidal. The credibility of such use, solo, against a Soviet leadership that was doing no more than seeking to impose its will on Europe by military force is low to vanishing' (p. 115). He also discounts the argument that the Polaris/Trident forces are an insurance against NATO breaking up: 'the same premium might be better invested in measures designed to prevent this happening rather than securing against it' (p. 116).

He concludes his critique of the effectiveness of Britain's

independent nuclear 'deterrent' with an extremely illuminating observation:

> Which brings us to the last and darkest, but probably the most fundamental reason why successive governments ever since World War II have sought and maintained an independent British strategic nuclear capability: they have seen it as vital to Britain's self esteem. In France this function of nuclear forces has always been both central and acknowledged. In the United Kingdom it lurks between the lines, and this is a pity, because the motive in itself is not ignoble. It is only a slight caricature to say that Polaris, having almost no possible military function, serves as a comparable prestige symbol to that of a loss-making national airline (p. 117).

This extraordinarily frank observation again suggests that 'deterrence' is not always the only, or even necessarily the most obvious, function of some nuclear weapons. In effect, this suggests that they have more a *political* than a military function. Further, for the ethicist, rather than for the military or for the politician, national 'self-esteem' might appear a most dubious justification for possessing such destructive weapons. In a situation of rapid nuclear proliferation many other countries will doubtless be keen to enhance their 'self-esteem' in a similar manner. There are presumably far safer ways for them to do that.

There are also ambiguities of function evident in MAD nuclear weapons as they exist at present. It has already been observed that both NATO and the Warsaw Pact possess amounts of such weapons far in excess of their possible use. If they were simply deterrents, rather than responses to nuclear expansion and proliferation, presumably they need exist in far fewer numbers. The very fact of their vast over-kill capacity is an indication that deterrence is not their only function.

If these arguments are accepted, it would seem that at three quite distinct levels – short-range nuclear weapons, British independent nuclear weapons and MAD nuclear weapons – the nuclear forces that exist at present cannot be unambiguously described as 'deterrents'. In each case other functions seem to be present; sometimes, perhaps, as their primary functions.

One moral response to this conclusion would be to criticize, and campaign to remove, those weapons which cannot be primarily justified as deterrents, whilst retaining those weapons which can be so justified. This would seem to be the overall position of Beach. Indeed, he even suggests that the possible removal of the not-wholly-deterrent nuclear weapons might be used as a means of negotiation in international discussions on nuclear arms reduction. But, of course, this position still assumes that some nuclear weapons do act as deterrents. Later chapters will discuss the morality of nuclear deterrence. For the moment it is important to focus upon the empirical question of the effectiveness of nuclear deterrence. On inspection, this too appears more problematic and less factual than might often be assumed.

A deterrent can only be a deterrent on someone or on some group of people who can be deterred. Clearly people who are mad or who feel they have nothing to lose cannot readily be deterred. Likewise, groups that cannot be caught cannot readily be deterred. For a deterrent to be effective there must normally be some perceived loss for the one to be deterred. Yet clearly the nuclear situation is fraught with such possibilities. As nuclear weapons continue to proliferate, so the chances increase that some mad leader, some terrorist group or some nation that feels that it has nothing to lose, will come to possess such weapons. In such situations the deterrent function of nuclear weapons soon evaporates. For many it appears to be only a matter of time before such situations arise.

Here is a central empirical weakness of so many assumptions about nuclear deterrence – assumptions that are evident throughout *The Cross and the Bomb.* They are framed in the context of the confrontation between NATO and the Warsaw Pact. Indeed, for the West, nuclear deterrence is overwhelmingly conceived in terms of deterring Soviet aggression. And, for the Soviet, nuclear deterrence is overwhelmingly conceived in terms of deterring the West and of deterring China. Nor surprisingly, these opposing conceptions feed each other: each side expands or 'modernizes' its nuclear weaponry in response to the other. But this very process tends to obscure dangers posed by the proliferation of nuclear weapons. Without underestimating Soviet fear or aggression (and, in the light of Afghanistan, it is crucial that this should be taken fully into consideration), the threat to nuclear peace posed by nuclear proliferation should be taken into greater account. Once it is, current strategies based upon bipolar nuclear deterrence appear less than adequate. Even Beach's discussion is written on the assumption of this bipolar strategy.

Bipolar nuclear deterrence is also problematic. The assumption is often made by the West (and *mutatis mutandis* by the Soviets) that Soviet aggression against the West has only been deterred in the last forty or so years by nuclear deterrence. Behind this assumption lie several antecedent assumptions. First, there is the assumption that the 'normal' relationship between the West and the Soviet is one of war, war which has only been prevented by nuclear deterrence – when, in fact, the Soviet have been British allies in both World Wars. Secondly, there is the assumption that it is indeed nuclear weapons, rather than non-nuclear weapons and memories of the appalling devastation caused by the latter in two World Wars, that have deterred Soviet aggression. And, thirdly, there is the assumption that countries can ultimately be 'deterred'. This final assumption is especially problematic. Sometimes a playground analogy is used. Graham Leonard, Keith Ward and Richard Harries all seek to justify social deterrence on the basis of examples taken from individual behaviour. Leonard uses the analogy of the mother and child: 'If a mother discovers her child stealing, her true love must include reproof based on recognition of the nature of the consequences of the act' (pp. 8f.). Ward and Harries also write about parents and children in the nuclear context: 'The parents who never discipline their children are not truly caring for them, or for what they may become' (Ward, pp. 49f.), and, 'A loving parent does not want a child to suffer the consequences of his carelessness by being run over' (Harries, p. 73). It was Reinhold Niebuhr who pointed out to Christians the fallacy of arguing about social issues from analogies drawn from individual behaviour, in his *Moral Man and Immoral Society* of 1932.[9] Sometimes the only actual use of nuclear weapons in war is cited as evidence that countries as well as individuals can be deterred. It is usually argued that, if the Japanese themselves already had possessed a nuclear bomb in 1945, the Americans would have been deterred from dropping their bombs. The force of this argument, however, is diminished somewhat if it is posed the other way around. On this version, it is asked whether, if the Japanese had possessed a nuclear bomb in 1945, they themselves would have used it against the Americans knowing that, in the process, they would be inviting the Americans to retaliate with a nuclear attack. This question raises the suspicion that there may well be countries which would, in desperation, engage in a mutually destructive nuclear first strike. Hitler might well have been prepared to do that had his scientists actually produced a nuclear bomb, and some of the Middle Eastern countries might be prepared to do that today.

At this point it is important to register caution. On several occasions the authors of *The Cross and the Bomb* express exasperation at the moral confidence of unilateralists. But, in turn, they have a tendency to express confidence in the empirical effectiveness of nuclear deterrence. In varying degrees, they admit moral doubts about certain aspects of nuclear weapons, but they are convinced that nothing should be done to weaken the nuclear deterrence which, they believe, has kept peace in Europe for forty years. They do not, of course, claim that nuclear weapons have kept peace in the world *tout court:* they are aware that there have been well over one hundred wars in the world since 1945, [10] quite undeterred by nuclear weapons. Yet, they are convinced that nuclear weapons are essential deterrents. The force of my argument so far is to attempt to express caution about such confident claims. It is far from clear that the primary function of all nuclear weapons is to act as deterrents. But, even when nuclear weapons are taken as a whole, it is still not clear whether or not nuclear weaponry can really act as an effective deterrent. In an area with so few precedents it is difficult to see how to resolve these empirical dilemmas. Yet the social consequences of conclusions that must eventually be reached in the political order are awesome.

If ambiguities abound at the empirical level of the nuclear debate, they exist in profusion at the moral level. Naturally, it is with the moral level that the authors of *The Cross and the Bomb* are primarily concerned. And it is this level which will form the substance of the rest of this book. In particular, it will seek to scrutinize four of the more strident claims made in varying degrees by the authors:

(*a*) that nuclear deterrence is not wrong in itself;

(*b*) that nuclear deterrence is not wrong in its consequences;

(*c*) that the use of certain nuclear weapons can be justified in terms of a Christian just-war theory;

(*d*) that unilateralism and 'nuclear pacifism' are morally irresponsible and, perhaps, even evil.

Before they are examined in detail, a number of initial points ought to be made about these four moral claims.

First, it should be stressed that they are significant claims. It is significant that this important group of churchmen and theologians are making them, and it seems reasonable to believe that their arguments will find a wider audience than might have been the case with less distinguished authors. But the claims themselves are also significant. They go beyond a straightforward moral defence of multilateralism to a defence of nuclear weapons as morally neutral and to an attack on their unilateral disavowal as morally defective. In the present volatile political climate of nuclear tension these are indeed signficant claims and merit careful scrutiny.

Secondly, the stridency with which these claims are made compares strikingly with other Christian discussions of nuclear issues. Few of the authors, with the exceptions of Ward and Beach, reflect the moral perplexity and caution so characteristic of the report, *The Church and the Bomb,* to which they are responding. The blurb of *The Cross and the Bomb* even suggests that the authors 'are united in their conviction that the trend towards unilateralism in the churches requires a robust response'. But, since their moral claims go beyond the position of a number of other Christians (who might not themselves normally be identified as pacifists), they again require careful scrutiny. If the volatile political climate is also taken into consideration here, it becomes particularly important that Christians should not legitimize positions on the nuclear issue which have not been subjected to such scrutiny. [11]

It is worth noting at this stage that recent theological

considerations of war have increasingly been characterized by a return to something like Augustine's regretful position. Although Augustine is usually remembered in this context as one of the first theologians to sanction warfare and to articulate a just-war theory (which will be the subject of Chapter 4), his arguments always started from a position of extreme regret and horror at war itself. The following passage illustrates this clearly:

> What is the evil in war? Is it the death of some who will soon die in any case, that others may live in peaceful subjection? This is mere cowardly dislike, not any religious feeling. The real evils in war are love of violence, revengeful cruelty, fierce and implacable enmity, wild resistance, and the lust of power, and such like; and it is generally to punish these things, when force is required to inflict the punishment that, in obedience to God or some lawful authority, good men undertake wars, when they find themselves in such a position as regards the conduct of human affairs, that right conduct requires them to act, or to make others act in this way (*Reply to Faustus the Manichaean XXII,* 69f., from *The Nicene and Post-Nicene Fathers,* Vol. 4).

This reluctance compares more than favourably with Aquinas' use of this very passage. Writing from the perspective of mediaeval Christendom, Aquinas[12] used Augustine simply to establish the criteria of a just war and ignored his expressions of horror at warfare itself. Even when he considered the reasons that might be advanced for suggesting that warfare is sinful, he reflected little of this horror:

> OBJECTIONS: 1. It would seem that it is always a sin to wage war. Punishments are meted out only for sin. But our Lord named the punishment for people who wage war when he said, 'All who draw the sword will die by the sword'. Every kind of war then is unlawful. 2. Moreover, whatever goes against a divine command is a sin. But war does that. Scripture says, 'I say this to you, offer the wicked man no resistance.' Also, 'Not revenging yourselves, my dearly beloved, but give place unto wrath.' War is always a sin then. 3. Besides, the only thing that stands as a contrary to the

act of virtue is a sin. Now war is the contrary of peace. Therefore it is always a sin. 4. Besides, if an action is lawful, practising for it would be lawful, as is obvious in the practice involved in the sciences. But warlike exercises which go on in tournaments are forbidden by the Church, since those killed in such trials are denied ecclesiastical burial. Consequently war appears to be plainly wrong (*Summa Theologica* 2a2ae.40.1, from the English Dominican translation, Vol. XXXV).

Aquinas then proceeded to refute these objections and to set out the necessary criteria for a just war. There is little room in his formalistic arguments to express any horror or personal distaste for warfare itself.

Although Paul Ramsey, perhaps the most influential Christian ethicist alive, can be just as formalistic at times, it is significant that his discussions of the morality of nuclear deterrence are always underpinned by a horror of the potentialities of nuclear destruction. Ramsey is a just-war theorist and does eventually support a policy of nuclear deterrence, but he is always careful to distinguish between the 'do-able' and the 'un-do-able' nuclear policies. In a highly instructive passage, he argues:

> None of the virtues of the limiting policy decisions for which a case can be made, or of war considered only in the context of constant massive deterrence, can invalidate the distinction between the do-able and the politically un-do-able. It is frequently contended that 'both prudence and international law' permit and make it 'desirable to carry out reprisals in kind', and that the only question remaining once an enemy strikes one of our cities is how to determine the equivalence to be exchanged moment by moment in countervalue war. Whatever may be the rule of reprisal in international law today, this can hardly be said to settle the question of the justice – the natural justice – of reprisal in kind (or in *some* kinds). If it is unjust for an enemy to destroy our society, the fact that he does or tries to do so first cannot make it any less of an injustice for us to destroy his . . . Such a law of reprisals can only be described as a product of an age of legal positivism where justice has become something men

and nations 'make'. No wonder they suppose they can make 'just' an act that before was 'unjust', or unjust when *first* done. With no sense of the difference between the do-able and the intrinsically un-do-able, the nations may well agree that a certain weapon or plan of war should never be used, unless, of course, it is. That excuse must today be called radically into question' (*The Limits of Nuclear War: Thinking About the Do-able and the Un-do-able,* The Council on Religion and International Affairs, 1963, p. 41).

This leads to my final point. It is essential to scrutinize the moral claims of *The Cross and the Bomb* in the light of the empirical facts about nuclear weapons that I have tried to set out in this chapter. I believe that an adequte moral account of the nuclear issue will take fully into account the existence, destructiveness, expansion, proliferation and instability of present-day nuclear weapons. I believe that it will also express some of the perplexity that I have set out about the empirical effectiveness of nuclear weapons as deterrents. Anything less would amount to a moral over-simplification. On such a dangerous issue, over-simplification could be literally disastrous.

2 *Is Nuclear Deterrence Wrong in Itself?*

The position of a possibly growing number of Christians might be summarized as follows: the possession of nuclear weapons, as they exist, is inherently evil and the intentional threat to use them is also evil, but, in a dangerous and often evil world, it would be even more evil to take precipitate action which might render their actual use by others more likely. On such an understanding, nuclear deterrence is viewed as the lesser of two evils. Of course, within these claims there are several assumptions which must be examined in later chapters. But in this chapter I intend to explore the claim that nuclear weapons, as they exist, are inherently evil, even if their possession might be seen, at present, as the lesser of two evils.

It is one of the more remarkable features of *The Cross and the Bomb* that this minimal claim is denied by several of its authors. Inconsistencies will be noticed later, but three of the authors, in particular, are concerned to deny that nuclear weapons are inherently evil. Dr Graham Leonard, Bishop of London and former Chairman of the General Synod's Board for Social Responsibility, rejects the contention of the Anglican Report that, 'the ethics of deterrence are the ethics of threatening to do something which one believes would be immoral, which one intends to do only in circumstances which will not arise because of the conditional threat' (*The Church and the Bomb,* p. 98). In contrast, Leonard claims that, 'a more accurate and less tendentious definition would be to say that the ethics of deterrence are the ethics of stating the consequences which would follow in certain circumstances, consequences which would be morally right though possibly not morally good, and which it is intended will not arise because the consequences have been made clear' (*The Cross and the Bomb,*

p. 18). Fr Gerard Hughes, SJ, head of philosophy and lecturer in ethics at Heythrop College, London University, concludes his discussion with the claim that, 'it cannot be shown in any important sense that possession of a deterrent is wrong in itself, or that the advocate of the deterrent is committed to forming an intention which is immoral' (p. 34). And Dr Francis Bridger, lecturer in social theology and ethics at St John's College, Nottingham, building directly on Hughes' claims, argues strongly against the 'overwhelming consensus' of Christians that 'nuclear weapons *per se,* and the possession of them even for purely deterrent purposes, are condemned. No Christian can properly accept their retention' (p. 40).

Leonard builds up his argument on the basis of a paradigm taken from law enforcement. He maintains that, 'we come face to face with the fact that it is frequently necessary to perform acts which it would be difficult to describe as morally good but which in the particular circumstance are right and permissible' (p. 17). To substantiate this distinction between morally 'good' actions, on the one hand, and morally 'right' or morally 'permissible' actions, on the other, he cites the example of the policeman who shoots in self-defence whilst attempting to enforce the law. In this case, 'the purpose of his action is not simply to defend himself. It is part of the process of demonstrating that the moral sanctions of society must be obeyed. His action cannot be described as morally good but it can, and I believe, must be defended as right and morally permissible' (p. 17). Leonard sees it as part of the fact that 'we do not live in an ideal world, in which the choices before us always present the possibility of actions which are morally good . . . in which none of the options open to us are [*sic*] wholly good and all have elements in them which we deplore' (p. 17). In facing such moral situations, he believes that, 'what we have to do is to consider the various courses open to us and to judge that one course, even though it may involve consequences which we would deplore, which we would certainly not describe as good and which we would certainly not intend, is that which we are under a moral obligation to pursue . . . I believe we can say that we are fulfilling our moral duty, though we may not be able to say that our actions are wholly morally good' (p. 18).

For Leonard, nuclear deterrence clearly fits this paradigm and can be described as morally 'right', morally 'permissible', and indeed as a moral 'obligation', even if it cannot actually be described as morally 'good':

> Whatever local sanctions may, from time to time, be effective in practice, the *ultimate* sanction for the preservation of peace and the resolution of disputes lies with the power of nuclear weapons which will not go away. There is no means by which a less appalling ultimate sanction can be substituted. Man by his ingenuity having devised such an ultimate sanction, his moral nature must be exercised in that context. He must not allow his own sinfulness to lead him to think that he can dispense with it and rely upon man's goodwill . . . It is for this reason that I do not believe that moral man can abandon the ultimate sanction for law and order nor deliver it into the hands of those who would have no moral scruples about its use' (p. 19).

In attempting to assess Leonard's argument it is important initially to see whether or not it takes fully into account the empirical facts about present-day nuclear weapons – their existence, destructiveness, expansion, proliferation and instability – and some of the perplexity about their effectiveness as deterrents, as set out in the previous chapter. He is clear about their existence and about the fact that they cannot be disinvented. His unwillingness to describe nuclear deterrence actually as morally 'good' indicates that he does take seriously the destructiveness of nuclear weapons. But there is little in his argument which acknowledges the facts about the expansion, proliferation and instability of present-day nuclear weapons. Indeed, the final claim in the quotation above shows that his argument is still tied to a bipolar nuclear situation in which nuclear weapons create, rather than undermine, world stability and international law and order. However, if it is the case that the rapid horizontal and vertical expansion of nuclear weapons and their continuing proliferation are actually contributing to their instability, then the force of Leonard's argument is seriously weakened. At every point in his argument, nuclear weapons are regarded as empirically (although not morally) unambiguous as deterrents.

These weaknesses alone are sufficient to make Leonard's argument questionable, but it also suffers from serious ethical deficiencies. Once again, the individualistic fallacy – arguing about social issues from analogies drawn from individual behaviour – seems to control his argument. To argue from the behaviour morally permissible for an individual policeman, acting in self-defence, to the behaviour of nations confronting each other in the nuclear situation is to commit an extraordinary category error in ethical analysis. Ironically, Leonard earlier seems to acknowledge as much when he quotes, with approval, Richard Harries' claim that, 'groups do not relate to one another in the same way as individuals do. The main difference lies in the fact that when relating to another individual I am dealing with someone who can, if he wishes, forego his own interests in favour of mine . . . But when two groups relate to one another neither is in a position to sacrifice its essential interests' (p. 10). In Chapter 5, I shall argue that it is a very elementary mistake (though frequently made) to argue about the morality of warfare on the basis of the morality of individual acts of violence.

Again, it is an obvious fallacy to argue from 'law and order' within a country to 'law and order' between countries. It may even be thoroughly misleading to use the same term, 'law and order', in these two quite different contexts. Here, too, Leonard is aware of an inconsistency. So he admits that 'we have to recognize that there is no system of international law and order with the means of its enforcement. There can, therefore, be no mechanism for the review and modification of sanctions by which law and order is presented and disputes resolved' (p. 19). Indeed, there are no universally recognized international police, there are no effective international sanctions for stopping all wars, and there are no effective means of enforcing or modifying such sanctions as do exist. In what sense, then, can the ethicist seriously equate the two situations? But, despite being aware of its obvious limitations, Leonard continues to use the analogy.

However, the most worrying feature of his argument for the ethicist is his attempt to distinguish between the morally 'right' (permissible) and the morally 'good'. It is significant that despite his use of this distinction, on several crucial occasions, [13] none of the other contributors adopts it. Of course, every ethicist must eventually try to make sense of situations of moral conflict. Moral conflicts generated by the nuclear issue are certainly not unique. But how an ethicist resolves such conflicts will depend largely upon which of three broad ethical approaches [14] he or she adopts.

The first approach (the subject of this chapter) might be termed the intrinsic ethical approach – or, to use its technical name, the deontological approach. Intrinsic ethical arguments are absolutist by nature: one cannot argue beyond them. So, if one maintains that murder is wrong and is asked to give a reason, an intrinsic ethical response would be: 'Because it is against the law of nature', or, 'Because it is against God's will', or, 'Because it breaks the Sixth Commandment', or even, 'Because it is simply wrong'. Such responses merely refer the other person to some norm or absolute beyond which there can be no further argument: murder is seen as wrong regardless of its consequences. Of course, there may be situations of moral ambiguity, but these the intrinsic ethicist will attempt to resolve, either by tighter definition, or by balancing competing moral claims. So many of those who believe that murder is wrong, but that killing in war can be justified, argue that the latter does not really involve the former (e.g. since war does not involve privately motivated killing). Others, attempting to balance competing moral claims, argue that, although killing in war is wrong, it is overridden by the greater wrong of not defending one's country when called upon to do so. It is this second mode of argument which is closest to that presented by Leonard in the nuclear context. Yet, there is a crucial difference. Whereas he attempts to distinguish between the morally 'right' and the morally 'good', this mode distinguishes rather between wrongs and greater wrongs.

The second approach (the subject of the next chapter) might be termed the consequential ethical approach – or, again to use its technical name, the teleological approach. Consequential ethical arguments treat morality, not as autonomous or as an end in itself, but as a means to something else. So, a consequentialist who believes that murder is wrong, might respond as follows: 'Because murder, if allowed, would destroy society', or, 'Because murder does not contribute to general happiness', or even, 'Because those who murder will receive eternal punishment in the next life'. In each response, murder is thought to be wrong, not because it is wrong in itself (the position of the intrinsic ethicist), but because it leads to something else which is thought to be wrong or perhaps just undesirable – e.g. the breakdown of society, the absence of general happiness, or the reception of eternal punishment. Thus, all moral conduct is judged in terms of its results or consequences. Moral conflict, for consequentialists, will consist less in situations of competing moral values or claims (which for them do not exist apart from consequences), than in situations wherein the consequences are either unclear or themselves in conflict. Those following this approach might argue, for example, that the happiness or well-being of society determines that the murder of all traitors is right and, indeed, 'good'. Intrinsic ethicists might argue that such murder is wrong (if indeed it is murder), but that it would be a greater wrong to allow one's country to be betrayed. There is a strong element of consequentialism in Leonard's argument (to which I shall return in the next chapter), although I suspect that his tendency is towards the intrinsic approach.

Some theorists distinguish a third ethical approach. This is sometimes termed a personalist or situational approach to ethics. [15] It is a feature of personalists that they view morality, not as obedience to autonomous, absolute principles or as a means to something else, but as an expression of individual feelings, conscience or love. It is an axiom of most personalists that moral dilemmas cannot be resolved in advance of particular situations. Thus, it makes no sense to argue, as an abstract principle, about whether or not murder is wrong. Only in particular situations, when the individual is confronted with the possibility of murder, can that individual determine whether or not it is wrong. Confronted with the prospect of murdering a particular individual now, the personalist might reply that this murder is wrong: 'Because I feel that it is wrong', or, 'Because my conscience tells me that it is wrong', or, 'Because it would contradict my love or respect for that person'. The emphasis in such responses is individualistic and situational: it is conceivable that, given a change in the situation or in the person to be murdered, the same individual might reach the conclusion that the murder is right. Further, a particular situation might involve the individual in a conflict between the competing demands of love, which must then be balanced against each other. The particular consequences of actions inherent within the situation might even be taken into consideration. But, there can be no *a priori* binding moral decisions about such issues as the justifiability of nuclear weapons (and thus no *a priori* clash between competing moral principles). The possession, or potential possession, of such weapons must be evaluated separately from case to case. Clearly, this is not Leonard's approach, or that of any of the other contributors to *The Cross and the Bomb.*

Each of these three ethical approaches, then, has a characteristically different method of resolving ambiguous moral situations. Leonard's argument does not seem to be entirely compatible with any of them. There is a strong consequentialist motif throughout, yet there does seem to be an overall commitment to intrinsic moral principles. Bridger sees it as a clear fault of many unilateralists, including the report *The Church and the Bomb,* that they simultaneously use both ethical approaches:

> The appeal to consequences cannot properly be made from an intrinsicalist standpoint. If it is wrong to have nuclear weapons *per se,* then they must be renounced, irrespective of consequences. The justification for renunciation likewise cannot be made by appeal to the importance of breaking log-jams and so on. They must be disposed of simply because they are in themselves evil, not because we believe their renunciation will have certain consequences. This major contradiction cannot be overlooked, and will give the questioning inquirer pause for thought about the coherence of the unilateralist case (p. 41).

I am not at all sure that this is the case or that these two ethical approaches (or the personalist third approach) are quite as separate and distinct as Bridger claims. It is neither contradictory nor incoherent to claim that nuclear weapons are inherently evil, but that it would be imprudent to ignore the potential consequences of their precipitate disposal. On a purely intrinsicalist approach, it is quite proper to argue that the possession of nuclear weapons is evil, but that their precipitate disposal would be even more evil. And many consequentialist approaches involve an eventual appeal to some intrinsic value. These are not exclusive or mutually inconsistent approaches. None the less, Bridger is quite correct to claim that clarity on the part of the ethicist about which approach is being adopted at which particular point in the argument does aid coherence. And, in this respect, Leonard remains ambiguous. Further, he does not seem to consider the possibility that nuclear deterrence is evil (as distinct from precipitate disposal which would be more evil) rather than right/permissible (as distinct from morally good).

One reason why he did not adopt this last possibility might be that he was already convinced that Gerard Hughes' article had successfully debunked it. It is Hughes' central aim to show that nuclear deterrence *per se* cannot properly be judged to be inherently evil or wrong. [16]

Hughes begins by considering the claim that 'possessing a deterrent is wrong in itself' and argues that: 'this claim is either question-begging or else simply unhelpful' (p. 29):

First, let me argue that, understood in one way, it is simply unhelpful. If we ask whether the *type* of action described by the phrase 'possessing a deterrent' is in itself right or wrong, surely the answer is that it is neutral, just as firing a gun is in itself neutral. If all we know about someone was that he possessed a deterrent, we would be unable to pass any moral judgement on what he was about. Merely to know that an action is of that type will be quite unhelpful from the moral point of view. To solve practical moral problems, one needs not merely to know about the morality of types of action; one needs also to know whether what is being done (or contemplated) really is an instance of that type; one needs to know of what other morally significant types of action it is also an instance; and one needs to have some overall method of assessing actions which instantiate several types at once (p. 29).

At this level of generality, Hughes' claims appear uncontentious. If one was to claim that the possession of any deterrent was wrong in itself, then one would have to regard the placing of locks on doors, walls around gardens and any other form of deterrent (against man or beast) as inherently wrong. Obviously, in order to form any serious moral judgment, one requires more empirical evidence. This Hughes provides by arguing next about the possession of a *nuclear* deterrent:

Suppose, then, that one is speaking about a particular case of possessing a nuclear deterrent – say, the present possession of such a deterrent by the Western Powers. Is that possession wrong in itself? I have already shown why this question cannot be solved merely by forming a moral view about the type of action 'possessing a deterrent' in itself, no matter what moral view that might be. Still less can it be solved if one thinks, as I do, that that type of action is in itself morally neutral. To solve the problem, one needs to know what other actions the Western possession of a nuclear deterrent instantiates. Is it, for example, also an instance of preventing a war? Is it an instance of greatly increasing the likelihood of war? If it is an instance just of the first, then this particular possession of a deterrent is surely right. If just of the second, equally surely it is wrong. But to decide which of these is actually the case requires . . . historical and political judgement . . . At this point, one would have to speak no longer as a moralist or a theologian, but as a historian or a politician. That our moral judgements should thus be at the mercy of other assessments to which as moralists we can make no privileged contribution may possibly seem most unfortunate. But morality is a practical science; and practical science cannot be carried out without actual investigation of the real world (pp. 29-30).

From this quotation it is evident that Hughes is a consequentialist. For him, the deciding factor on the morality of the possession of nuclear deterrence is whether it results in the prevention of war or in the increased likelihood of war. In so far as such consequential judgments depend upon empirical conclusions about the effectiveness or non-effectiveness of nuclear weapons as deterrents, the ethicist is indeed dependent on historical and political judgments. But a discussion of this must wait until the next chapter.

However, this does not resolve the issue. Hughes believes that it does and claims:

> It follows that to assert that possession of the deterrent is in itself immoral will either be to make a theoretical remark (and I believe an implausible one at that) with no practical bearing on the particular instance of the possession of the deterrent by the Western Powers; or else it will be a somewhat misleading way of summarizing a lengthy historical and political study – which is why the phrase 'in itself' is out of place (p. 30).

But his argument only appears plausible because it is stated in the most abstract of terms. In the conclusion just quoted he refers first to 'possession of *the* deterrent'. Yet, in the argument quoted earlier, he refers only to 'possessing *a* deterrent' – and, of course, has little difficulty in showing that possessing *a* deterrent (presumably just *any* deterrent) can hardly be inherently wrong. From this it is but a short step to claim that 'possessing *a* nuclear deterrent' can hardly be inherently wrong. And from this it appears to follow that '*the* possession of *the* deterrent by *the* Western Powers' today can hardly be inherently wrong. The casual substitution of an odd word or two soon produces conviction. Thus, the remarkable conclusion is soon reached that the possession of nuclear weapons is a morally neutral form of activity – it is only the use to which they are put that can be morally wrong.

It is precisely at this point that a rather crucial inconsistency is evident amongst the contributors to *The Cross and the Bomb*. By no means are they all convinced about the moral neutrality of possessing nuclear weapons or even about the moral status of using them as deterrents. Keith Ward, the F. D. Maurice Professor of Moral and Social Theology at King's College, London University, does appear to regard the nuclear situation as inherently evil. He argues that there are situations of moral dilemma in which 'there are conflicts of duty, where you cannot avoid doing something that is, in general, wrong' and in which 'there is no possibility of avoiding evil' (p. 52). He continues:

> In the case of nuclear deterrence, there is just such a moral dilemma; indeed, just about the worst one conceivable. The dilemma is that, on the one hand, you ought not to threaten, or seem to threaten, however conditionally, to destroy millions of innocent people by massive nuclear attack. But, on the other hand, you ought not to allow a tyrannical and oppressive regime to attack and conquer your country, if you have a means of preventing it. If this is right . . . then, whatever you do will be in breach of some great duty. I think it is important to stress this, for there are absolutists who hold that real dilemmas never occur, and that it is always possible not to do evil, whatever the consequences. In this world, on the contrary, there are times when one has to do something evil, to prevent a greater evil. There is no choice. Whichever way we choose, we are doing evil to prevent evil. The only possible reply to this would be to say that permitting a great and avoidable evil was not a case of doing evil. That would, I think, be word-play of the worst sort. For permitting evil is wrong, if it is avoidable; therefore such permitting is a form of doing wrong, even if it consists of sitting still' (p. 52-3).

This unambiguous passage stands in odd contrast to the other contributions already reviewed in this chapter. Nuclear deterrence does seem to be regarded as evil 'in itself' (albeit as an evil to prevent a greater evil) and alternative positions are dismissed as 'word-play of the worst sort'.

This frank admission seems to be made possible by identifying nuclear deterrence as the threat, or apparent threat, 'however conditionally, to destroy millions of innocent people by massive nuclear attack'. That is, the possession of nuclear weapons is seen as *inherently* evil and destructive – a consideration quite independent of consequential conclusions about their role in preventing war or in increasing its likelihood. Now, if this depiction of nuclear deterrence is substituted in Hughes' argument for his abstract terms, much of his apparent plausibility is lost. It might now read as follows:

Suppose, then, that one is speaking about a particular case of threatening, or seeming to threaten, however conditionally, to destroy millions of innocent people by massive nuclear attack. Is that wrong in itself? I have already shown why this question cannot be solved merely by forming a moral view about this type of action in itself, no matter what moral view that might be. Still less can it be solved if one thinks, as I do, that that type of action is in itself morally neutral . . .

Nor does the ethicist require the special skills of the historian or the politician in order to depict 'nuclear deterrence' in this way. He need only frame the argument in less abstract terms.

Hughes' abstraction disguises another significant point. It emerges that his argument is not concerned solely with deterrence in general, or even with nuclear deterrence in general, but with present-day Western nuclear deterrence. Once this point is discerned, the empirical facts about present-day nuclear weapons, which I have already sought to identify, again become relevant. Hughes is certainly aware of the existence and destructiveness of these weapons, but nowhere mentions their expansion, proliferation and instability. Yet (if my analysis is correct) any serious ethical account of Western nuclear deterrence, as it exists today, should take them into consideration – quite apart from any consideration of the supposed consequences of this deterrence. And, once they *are* taken into consideration, it becomes even more difficult to claim that the possession of present-day nuclear weapons is 'morally neutral'. It is difficult to see that possessing such extraordinarily dangerous weapons, which are fast expanding horizontally and vertically, which are proliferating from one country to another, and which are becoming increasingly unstable, can be considered to be anything but inherently evil.

It is one of the ironies of *The Cross and the Bomb* that some of the theologians who are insisting that Christians have a special reason to recognise frankly the reality of evil in the world and to combat it responsibly with a nuclear deterrent are themselves so resistant to recognizing that the possession of nuclear weapons is itself inherently evil. Of course they might then use consequential arguments to show that these weapons should not be abandoned precipitately. But that would not alter a prior judgment that the possession of nuclear weapons, as they exist in the world today, is indeed evil. Christians do have special reasons for believing that such deadly weapons demonstrate the reality of not only evil but also human sin. Their very existence is the product of quite deliberate and sustained scientific effort, which might have been channelled into sustaining and nourishing a hungry world. Their unsurpassed destructiveness has made a man-made Armageddon an actual possibility and has succeeded in transposing transcendent theological concepts of apocalypse into this-wordly political options. Their vertical expansion has ensured that an ever-increasing amount of God-given resources, in a world of finite resources, must be spent on the pursuit of nuclear deterrence. Their horizontal expansion has ensured that a nuclear option is present at every serious level of future military confrontation between East and West. Their continuing proliferation means that the least responsible political leaders and nations in the world are themselves moving towards nuclear possession. And their increasing instability means that all of these possibilities may soon become realities. Even if nuclear weapons are eventually accepted, with deep reluctance, as barriers against human sin, their very possession inextricably involves their inventors, manufacturers, distributors and possessors in sin.

It might be argued that any understanding of the possession of nuclear weapons which does not acknowledge this deep and inherent sinfulness is less than Christian. However strongly Christians may feel about some of the more simplistic defences of unilateralism and however emphatic they are to see justice done to the cause of multilateralism, in the interests of world safety, they should not ignore these dimensions of human sin. To claim that the possession of nuclear weapons, as they exist in the world today (let alone their actual use), is 'morally neutral' or even 'morally right', might be judged by some as distinctly sub-Christian. Quite apart from anything else, such claims may provide their political possessors and ultimate users with a fearful legitimation. This is a heavy responsibility for theologians to carry.

3 *Is Nuclear Deterrence Wrong in its Consequences?*

The reluctant justification of nuclear deterrence, which opened my previous chapter, sought to combine intrinsic and consequential ethical approaches. From an intrinsic perspective, it was claimed that the possession of nuclear weapons is inherently evil and that the intentional threat to use them is also evil. From a consequential perspective, it was claimed that, in a dangerous and often evil world, it would be even more evil to take any precipitate action which might render the actual use in war of nuclear weapons by others more likely. It will be the aim of this chapter to examine the assumptions lying behind this second perspective.

Amongst these assumptions the following are the most important. First, there is an assumption that the world is indeed dangerous and often evil. A number of the contributors to *The Cross and the Bomb* link this assumption to the theological concept of the Fall. Secondly, there is an assumption that the possession of nuclear weapons does act as a deterrent in such a world. Thirdly, there is an assumption that the peace resulting from the use of nuclear weapons as a deterrent provides a consequential moral justification of their possession. And fourthly, there is an assumption that a precipitate disposal of nuclear weapons (i.e. unilateralism) might result in a greater likelihood of their use than would their retention and, accordingly, must be judged consequentially to be morally wrong. Although these assumptions are obviously interlinked, it is nevertheless important, for the sake of clear analysis, to scrutinize them separately.

The concept of the Fall occupies a pivotal position in Graham Leonard's argument. He starts his article by summarizing what he sees as the biblical understanding of the Fall:

In the Prologue in Genesis, certain basic characteristics of man
are established. He is given the power of choice whether to obey
God or not. That choice involves the recognition of the
difference between good and evil. The exercise of that choice in a
way which does not accord with the will of God has the gravest
consequences. Man is isolated from God and from his fellow
men. Conflict arises and man is pictured as trying to build for
himself a civilization which would justify itself apart from God
and the result of which is chaos and confusion. Man who as
viceregent of creation is called upon to express the praises of
creation to its Creator finds himself in a world which was
'corrupt before God' and 'filled with violence'. It is in that
context that man is still called upon to exercise his power of
choice, discerning what is good and what is evil and cleaving to
the good (pp. 5-6).

Leonard sees the final book in the Christian Bible as the Epilogue
in which, 'we are given a vision of the ultimate purpose for which
creation exists. It is the gathering together of all things in one in
Christ. The whole of creation, freed from the bondage of
corruption, perfectly fulfils itself and does so to the glory of God . . .
But it also makes clear in the most dramatic way that this can only be
achieved by the defeat of evil, with which there can be compromise'
(p. 6). Between this Prologue and Epilogue, 'man exists in a fallen
world: in Old Testament times with the promise of salvation and
since Pentecost with salvation achieved but still to be implemented.
In both ages he exists in a world which, being disordered, needs an
authority to restrain, an authority which must ultimately be backed
by power to secure justice and freedom' (p. 6). He believes that
neither the Old Testament nor the New Testament condemns such
authority: 'On the contrary in the Old Testament the authority and
power of Cyrus, King of Persia, was, for example, used by God in
the preparation of the people of Israel for the coming of Christ; in
the New Testament the authority of Caesar is recognized both by
Our Lord and in the Epistles' (pp. 6-7).

It cannot be denied that there is a strong emphasis upon sin in
both the Old Testament and the New Testament. Indeed, any valid

understanding of the nuclear issue in Christian ethics must take human frailty and sin fully into account. None the less, there are difficulties involved in accepting Leonard's version of 'salvation history'. Many biblical scholars today would be hesitant about producing a harmonized version of 'the biblical understanding' of an issue, such as that of power and authority. Instead, they might point to some of the discontinuities between the Old Testament and the New Testament.[17] If this is not done, some very curious moral positions seem to emerge. For example, if the power of Cyrus is seen as a product of God, then presumably it was indeed God who first hardened the heart of Pharaoh' (Ex. 14.4) and then drowned him (Ex. 14.26), and it was God who 'destroyed the nations' whose land the Israelites had come to occupy (Deut. 8.20). Such exegesis soon produces a number of sub-Christian positions. Keith Ward even argues that, 'Evil will be conquered by the power of God; and that God is the same Lord of Hosts who was with the people of Israel in battle, and who delivered them from Egypt by drowning the Egyptian' (p. 48). And, a little later, having taken the example of parents exercising discipline over their children, he writes that 'I am not suggesting that parents should kill or maim very naughty children', but adds immediately, in parentheses, 'though see Deuteronomy 21' (p. 50). Presumably he is referring to Deut. 21.18-21, but he cannot seriously be hinting that there is anything remotely 'Christian' about that passage.

In addition to these exegetical problems (to which I shall return in Chapter 5), a position in Christian ethics based upon notions of the Fall has other difficulties. These might be illustrated by analysing Francis Bridger's somewhat different understanding of the Fall. He bases his argument (perhaps unwisely) on Reinhold Niebuhr's famous defence of Western democracy in *The Children of Light and the Children of Darkness* (Nisbet 1945):

> Our assessment of Western values will . . . inevitably come back to our doctrine of man. He is made in the image of God with creativity and freedom, but he is flawed. The Fall has not destroyed the divine image in men, but it has marred it. Consequently human life is highly ambiguous. In the redemptive

plan of God, these contradictions will ultimately be resolved. But until that eschatological fulfilment, our social organization must recognize the tension between what God would have us to be and what we, as men, actually are. Western democracy with its understanding of the need for checks and balances of power represents a better approximation (however rough) to Christian realism than does Soviet totalitarianism (p. 44).

The attempted balance reflected in the statement that the Fall 'has not destroyed the divine image in men, but it has marred it' has been the subject of centuries of theological debate.[18] Despite the confidence with which Bridger makes it, it is clearly but one attempt. It is also fairly close, at this period of his life, to Niebuhr's own understanding of the Fall. So, in the published version of his Gifford lectures, he argued that the Fall, properly understood, involves sin that is 'a corruption of man's true essence but not its destruction' (*The Nature and Destiny of Man*, Vol. 1, Nisbet 1941, p. 285). But Niebuhr was fully aware that the very notion of the Fall presented theologians with a major difficulty, once they ceased to hold the 'literalistic error of insisting upon the Fall as an historical event' (p. 284):

> One of the consequences of this literalism, which has seriously affected the thought of the church upon the problem of man's essential nature, is the assumption that the perfection from which man fell is to be assigned to a particular historical period, i.e. the paradisaical period before the Fall . . . The effect of this literalism has been to bring confusion into Christian thought on the relation of man's essential nature to his sinful condition. In Protestant thought it aggravated the tendency toward extravagant statements of man's depravity . . . In Catholic thought, chronological literalism encouraged the definition of the state of original righteousness as a special supernatural gift . . . which was added to . . . the essential humanity which Adam had as man (pp. 284-5).

Niebuhr was wrestling with one of the most intractable dilemmas in Christian theology – attempting to assess the state of human nature *vis à vis* God. It is hardly surprising that, in the course of his own life, he somewhat changed the balance. There is even a discrepancy between the lectures, as they were originally delivered, on this issue, and as they eventually appeared, in print (originally they were more inclined towards the Protestant tendency). This is an issue which has always divided Christians and, with the fresh division between those who accept and those who reject the historicity of the Fall, continues to divide them.

Richard Harries, the Dean of King's College, London, does appear to be more aware than others of these divisions amongst Christians and of the dilemmas raised by Niebuhr. He recognizes that 'some modern people find it impossible to make sense of assertions such as "man is fallen" or else they are alienated by such language' (p. 76). So, although he himself appears to accept the language of the Fall, he devotes most of his article to more secular analysis of the human condition. His central points are that, 'coercion is necessary because human beings pursue their own interests, they have only a limited capacity to transcend those interests for a greater good, and in organized group life these tendencies become normative' (p. 76). Further, his defence of Western democracy is distinctly more muted than that of Bridger. He argues explicitly against those who 'talk about defending Christian civilization or Christian values against atheistic communism' (p. 75). Adopting a more Lutheran position, he maintains that, 'though civilization of all kinds can and should be defended against forces which seek to destroy them, what is distinctively Christian cannot and should not be so defended . . . What has to be defended are the conditions which make human life of any kind possible. The good has to be freely chosen but the conditions which make it possible for the good to be chosen have to be maintained. These conditions cannot be upheld simply on the basis of goodwill; coercion is necessary both within states and between them' (p. 75). Although this (characteristically Lutheran[19]) defence of 'civilizations *of all kinds*' has obvious weaknesses, it does present a clear understanding of the nature of and necessity for social coercion. What it does not demonstrate is the necessity for nuclear coercion.

So much of Harries' article is taken up by a discussion of coercion in general that it is only in the last few pages that he considers Christian positions. It becomes evident that his defence of nuclear weapons is entirely consequential:

> One of the prime functions of government is to defend its people. Those who are elected to office in it are expected, rightly, to fulfil this function. A government that neglects this function is being not just foolish but immoral . . . It would be immoral, for example, for a Christian statesman to renounce a particular weapon if he genuinely believed that the weapon enhanced the defence of the realm or if he thought that holding on to the weapon would enable an agreement to be made with an adversary power which would bring real reductions in their weapons. That politician, as a Christian individual, might be tempted to make a moral gesture by renouncing the weapon . . . Nevertheless, as a politician in government it would be immoral . . . His main concern therefore will always be with the practical consequences of suggested decisions. Will it or will it not have the desired effect? And this, despite all eschewing of moral gestures (unless they are calculated to serve a specific and predicted purpose) is a highly moral endeavour (pp. 84-5).

There is obvious good sense in much of this argument. Few would deny that it is a prime function of government to defend its people. Further, most might insist that, at least in a democracy, it is for politicians to serve the people and that, unless the latter have themselves renounced arms, politicians must be prepared to sanction the use of arms in defence of the people. But, again, Harries seems to have overstated his position. Can *any* and *every* weapon be so sanctioned? And should *any* and *every* state or nation (not always an easy distinction to make) be so defended? Pure consequentialism can lead to some very curious moral conclusions.

Returning to Paul Ramsey's arguments (see the end of Chapter 1), Harries makes no distinction between the politically 'do-able' and the politically 'un-do-able' and contains no concept of 'justice'. For Ramsey, 'if it is unjust for an enemy to destroy our society, the fact that he does or tries to do so first cannot make it any less of an injustice for us to destroy his . . . Such a law of reprisals can only be described as a product of an age of legal positivism where justice has become something men and nations "make" ' (*The Limits of Nuclear War,* 1963, p. 41). In an (uncharacteristically) impassioned passage in an earlier book[20] he wrote:

The fact of the matter is that, eschewing pre-emptive war and conceding the first strike, the supposed deterrent effect of our great weapons lies in our second-strike capability alone, or in such capability as will remain after the first strike. Since this is known well enough to any potential enemy, and since our capability to deliver unacceptable damage to him after receiving the first strike is dubious indeed, wherein now lies the deterrence? . . . In any case, nothing in the present world situation can provide sufficient reason for altering radically the very meaning of *ratio* even in a nation's appeal to *ultima ratio* of war, least of all for Christians who have come to an understanding of what is reasonable and just in the conduct of war only from a love-transformed justice and a faith illuminated by reason. To this they would tempt us whose moral premises are so thin as to lead logically to the verdict which justifies most of all that act of war which will be the most immoral, because the most stupid and politically purposeless, in the whole history of warfare, namely, the unleashing of counter-nuclear retaliation by means of push-buttons . . . To press the button in counter-retaliation will also be the most unloving deed in the history of mankind, only exceeded by those who, for the sake of some concern of theirs, cause the little ones to stumble and fall into hell. I had rather be a pagan suckled in a creed outworn, terrified at the sight of hands made impure by any shedding of blood, than a skilful artisan of technical reason devising plans to carry out such a deed' (*War and the Christian Conscience: How Shall Modern War be Conducted Justly?,* Duke University 1961, pp. 169-70).

Without some concept of 'justice' (to which I shall return in the next chapter), purely consequentialist ethical justifications of nuclear deterrence risk legitimating the most appalling political expedients. The only relevant criterion becomes whether or not particular politicians imagine that particular weapons are necessary for defence. Ramsey likens this to a policy of tying babies to car bumpers in order to deter people from driving dangerously! More practicably, if it could be shown that introducing capital punishment for speeding offenders reduced drastically the number of innocent people killed on the road, a purely consequentialist approach might conclude that it was indeed justified. Capital punishment would hopefully act as a sufficient deterrent to ensure both that innocent victims were spared and that punishable speeders became a rarity! Some notion of 'justice' seems to be required to avoid such moral nonsense, and it is significantly missing from Harries' argument. Without this, the theologian can easily become a dangerous legitimator of nuclear expediency and, in effect, the notion of the Fall can become a licence to sin.

A full acknowledgment of the empirical facts about present-day nuclear weapons sharpens this point. Once it is questioned whether these weapons, as they actually exist, really do all have an unambiguous deterrent function, and once it is realized that they are expanding horizontally and vertically, continuously proliferating and becoming increasingly unstable, some concept of 'justice' becomes even more imperative. If this really is the present nuclear situation, it can hardly be the proper role of theologians to act as legitimators of the nuclear *status quo.* After more than twenty years, Ramsey's agitation appears as relevant as ever.

There are two important ways of avoiding some of these dilemmas. The first of these depends upon a notion of deterrence by bluff and the second upon a notion of a wholly effective deterrent. So, if it is claimed that an effective possession of a nuclear deterrent must involve an immoral intention actually to use it if necessary, either of these notions shows that this need not be the case. In the case of nuclear bluff, it is conceded that nuclear deterrence need involve only an *apparent* intention to use it. In the case of wholly effective nuclear deterrence, it is claimed that the possession of the deterrent will ensure that it never in fact has to be used. In either case, the possession of nuclear weapons ensures the morally desirable consequence of international peace, without the morally undesirable risk of nuclear war.

In theory, both of these options provide valid consequential justifications of nuclear deterrence. But, in practice, both must face very serious empirical weaknesses.

On the first option, Ramsey proved to be his own critic. In *The Limits of Nuclear War* he argued that, 'any politically viable solution of the problem of war today requires that we finally employ a distinction between the *possibility* and the *certainty* of illimitable city destruction; and in deterrence during the war that we carefully discriminate between the *appearance* and the *actuality* of being partially or totally committed to go to city exchanges . . . A nation ought never to be totally committed to action that is so irrational it can never be done by free, present decision; and even to *appear* to be totally committed may itself be altogether too dangerous. A nation ought not to communicate to an enemy that it might go to city exchanges without at the same time communicating some doubt about it, if it wants both to remain and to seem to remain a free agent with still some control over its destiny and the course of world politics. The *appearance* of *partial* commitment, or the *appearance* of *possible* commitment, may be enough of a commitment to deter an enemy' (p. 43). But, in the earlier *War and the Christian Conscience* he had already conceded that, 'an enemy cannot know what he has to fear unless he also knows what he has not to fear, and (what is more important) he cannot translate power into policy without letting him know. He will probe anyway, and find out. In politics, there is perhaps some usefulness in bluffing about the weapons we may or may not possess, but very little usefulness in bluffing about what we intend or are willing to do with the weapons we are known to have' (p. 166).

In *The Cross and the Bomb* Gerard Hughes takes the bluff option seriously and sees that it avoids some of the problems facing other theories of nuclear deterrence. None the less, he too concedes that, 'for the nuclear deterrent as we know it to succeed, it is in practice essential that many of the personnel involved in the chain of command should quite clearly intend to fire their weapons if ordered. It would be in practice impossible for all these people to be merely bluffing without this fact eventually becoming public knowledge. And once it is public knowledge, the deterrent loses much, if not all, of its credibility' (p. 31). In such a situation, one of the obvious dangers is the possibility of a mistake. Even if the few at the top are clear that nuclear deterrence ultimately depends upon bluff (and, to an extent, it does), and even if one could be confident that their successors will be similarly convinced, [21] if those lower down are themselves unaware of this (as they must be), misunderstandings eventually might arise. Of course, the fact that any such misunderstanding has not yet resulted in a nuclear release mitigates this. Yet the horizontal and vertical expansion of nuclear weapons today may seem to render the chances of such a misunderstanding occurring, at some time, more than a theoretical possibility. If the still relatively crude computers that form essential roles in the chain of communication (stage five computers have yet to be developed in this context) are also taken into consideration, the present situation appears even more dangerous. [22] Bluff, especially when the stakes are high, tends to be a dangerous pursuit.

Hughes does not regard the fact that some personnel in the nuclear chain of command really do intend to use the weapons, if necessary, as a fatal flaw in deterrence theory. He maintains that, 'there is no logical relationship between the intention to use the deterrent formed in circumstances where only having that intention will in fact ensure that it need never be used, and the intention to use the deterrent in circumstances where it has already failed' (p. 33). It is here that the second deterrence theory, that based upon a wholly effective nuclear deterrent, is evident. It is, indeed, perfectly logical to claim that there is a difference between someone who intends to use nuclear weapons, but who knows that this very intention will ensure that they never have to be used, and someone else who intends to use such weapons even if it can be shown that they are not wholly effective deterrents.

Unfortunately Hughes weakens the argument by writing sometimes about an intention which 'will in fact ensure' that nuclear weapons 'need never be used' and sometimes about intentions which merely make 'such a war less likely'. So, he claims that 'it is no doubt paradoxical that only by maintaining a credible deterrent is it possible to make nuclear war less likely, and that the more convincing the preparations the less likely that they will ever be called into action. But this paradox, if it is one, is not somehow a failure in the logic of intention, it is a peculiarity of the historical situation in which we are placed. The intentions of well-informed agents acting in these circumstances will reflect the complexity of their situation' (p. 33). But there *is* a clear moral difference between this situation and that based upon a wholly effective nuclear deterrent. One based upon a nuclear deterrent which will always deter will never involve its possessor in doing the 'un-do-able'. But this other situation might entail doing the 'un-do-able'. The risk is always there.

And, indeed, there are strong reasons for believing that the risk *is* always there and that a 'wholly effective nuclear deterrent' is simply a theoretical construct. Not only is the possibility of accidental use a problem in this context, but there are also the outstanding questions raised in Chapter 1 about the empirical effectiveness, as deterrents, of present-day nuclear weapons. Apparently Hughes believes that it is for the politician and the historian, not for the theologian, to make judgments about such empirical issues. He is concerned solely with the moral issue:

> The advocate of the deterrent policy will [*sic*] believe that only if here and now he fully intends to use it will the deterrent succeed in preventing war. That belief . . . will rest on a historical and political judgement which could, of course, turn out to be mistaken. Still, given that he holds that belief, the advocate of the deterrent will certainly say that he fully intends to use nuclear weapons should he be attacked. In so saying he is not, I think, logically committed to give the same answer in the quite different situation which would obtain if he were attacked. In that situation, indeed, it is most unlikely that he would be asked. But until he is asked *in those circumstances,* he need say nothing different from what he will say at the moment (p. 34).

Hughes has reached this extraordinary conclusion, first, by distinguishing sharply between judgments that it is proper for a

theologian to make and those which must be left for the historian or
politician, and then, by dividing the possessors of nuclear weapons
into two quite distinct camps –one consisting of those who believe
that nuclear weapons are wholly effective deterrents and the other
consisting of those confronted by a situation in which it is shown
that sadly they are not. Of course, it is important to make distinctions
in ethical analysis, but to make them at the expense of the realities of
the present-day nuclear situation is manifestly absurd. Any
responsible theologian, attempting to make sense of the nuclear
situation today, *must* make empirical judgments. Naturally, it is to
be hoped that he or she will have the humility to realize that they are
fallible judgments and will have the intelligence to make them
informed judgments. But to leave them uncritically for the 'experts'
to make would be an act of extraordinary moral irresponsibility. In
Chapter 6 I will argue that it is precisely through persistent moral
probing, even in areas of such empirical complexity, that the
theologian can seek to change the moral stances of the 'experts'.

In my arguments so far, I have attempted to throw doubt upon
some of the assumptions contained within consequential
justifications of nuclear deterrence, outlined at the beginning of this
chapter. I have questioned the central assumption that the resultant
peace from the use of nuclear weapons as a deterrent provides a
moral justification of their possession. I have raised doubts again
about whether present-day nuclear weapons really do function
unambiguously as deterrents. And I have claimed that
consequential justifications of nuclear weapons ought to be
tempered by some notion of 'justice' and of some notion of what is
'do-able' and what is 'un-do-able' in any future war. But I have yet
to test the final assumption that a precipitate disposal of nuclear
weapons might result in a greater likelihood of their use and,
accordingly, must be judged consequentially to be morally wrong.

Chapter 5 will consider in detail the morality of 'nuclear
pacifism'. Nevertheless, it can be admitted at this stage that it is
important, especially on such a crucial issue, that the ethicist takes
fully into account the world as it is and not the world as the ethicist
thinks that it ought to have been like. Nuclear weapons already exist
and cannot be disinvented. Further, they may already be in the

possession of those who care little about whether or not they are morally justifiable. So, even if the ethicist concludes that the possession of nuclear weapons as they currently exist is inherently evil, and that their supposed function as deterrents is morally questionable, he or she may still hesitate to recommend their immediate disposal. Such hesitancy scarcely amounts to a full-bodied moral justification of their possession. But it does make an important concession to the dangers of the present-day nuclear situation. A concession of this type has been made both by Pope John Paul II and by the World Council of Churches (see Chapter 6).

However, even this concession needs to be qualified. First, it should be stressed that the nuclear *status quo* is changing fast and changing in a potentially dangerous manner. Once again, if it is seen that nuclear weapons are expanding, proliferating and becoming increasingly unstable, then it will be evident that the *status quo* itself is fraught with danger. So, even if the unilateral disposal of nuclear weapons is finally deemed to be too dangerous and precipitate, their continued maintenance is hardly a safe option. The ethicist is left to choose between two opposing options, both of which appear to be potentially extremely dangerous, with no clear precedents to guide this choice.

Secondly, there must be some doubt about whether mankind can finally be trusted with possessing so many nuclear weapons. Leaving aside arguments about the Fall, if the general assumption of the contributors to *The Cross and the Bomb* about the extent of human sin is accepted, the conclusions that are derived from this assumption can be partially reversed. In one way or another they conclude that, if mankind is so sinful and in such need of social coercion, then nuclear deterrents are essential. Indeed, they see nuclear pacifism as the product of a falsely optimistic picture of people and nations. But, of course, it is also possible for those who argue from a unilateralist perspective to maintain in addition, that it is precisely their acknowledgment of human sinfulness and frailty which leads them to believe that mankind is not to be trusted with nuclear weapons. For them, human sinfulness requires as fast a reduction in nuclear arms as is possible. So, even whilst admitting that nuclear weapons cannot be disinvented, they might still maintain that the existence of so many and such a variety of weapons places an enormous temptation before sinful humanity. The argument comes full circle. The very assumptions which underpin this consequential justification of nuclear deterrence become a basis of its critique.

The previous chapter concluded with the contention that nuclear weapons involve their inventors, manufacturers, distributors and possessors inextricably in sin. This chapter concludes with the suggestion that a frank acknowledgment of the extent of human sin may lead to the belief that mankind is not to be trusted with the current levels of nuclear weapons. In moral terms, the possession of nuclear weapons is regarded, first as wrong in itself and, second, as wrong in its consequences. In the next chapter I must consider whether the actual use of nuclear weapons can ever be morally justified.

4 *Can the Use of Nuclear Weapons Ever be Justified?*

Few of the contributors to *The Cross and the Bomb* consider the question of whether or not the actual use of nuclear weapons in war ever can be justified. For most of them it is sufficient that nuclear weapons act as powerful deterrents in a sinful world. However, unless one holds, either that nuclear deterrence ultimately depends upon bluff, or that it ensures that nuclear war will in fact never occur (and I have raised doubts about both of these theories), then questions concerning the actual use in war of nuclear weapons should not be ignored. For Christians, the question of the moral justifiability of particular methods of warfare has, for many centuries, been considered to be extremely important. Since Augustine, there has been a long tradition of attempting to distinguish between 'just' and 'unjust' methods and types of war. Once it is admitted that the possession of an effective nuclear deterrent does involve (however remotely) the possible release of nuclear weapons in war, the relevance of this tradition becomes evident. Thus it becomes important to ask whether or not any potential use (or the two past actual uses) of any nuclear weapon in war is consonant with traditional just-war theory.

Gerard Hughes does not discuss directly the morality of using nuclear weapons in warfare, but rather concedes 'for the sake of the discussion that the actual use of nuclear weapons is wrong' (p. 31). None the less this does not represent his own position. He hints that the contention 'that any and every use of nuclear weapons is clearly morally wrong . . . is either an unwarranted generalization which ignores the differences between various types of weapon; or else it takes as obvious what I would have thought was a more disputable point, that the use of any nuclear weapon will inevitably lead to the use of any available type of nuclear weapon' (p. 31). These hints highlight some of the empirical difficulties facing a discussion of the morality of using present-day nuclear weapons.

Many of these empirical difficulties can be clustered around the concept of nuclear escalation. If it can be shown that the use of any nuclear weapon in war will lead to wholesale nuclear escalation, then it matters little what type of nuclear weapon actually started this process. Even if it appears just 'likely' (to use a weaker term than Hughes allows) that such escalation will follow any use, it matters little that weapons should be so distinguished. Only if it is just 'possible' that escalation will follow does it become important to assess whether particular weapons might make this possibility more or less remote.

Unfortunately the experts appear to be divided on the issue of nuclear escalation. [23] Even within *The Cross and the Bomb* opinions appear to differ between the civil servant, Michael Quinlan, and the former soldier, Hugh Beach. Quinlan argues that NATO policy is not based on 'winning' even a limited nuclear war. He points out that, 'the destruction in even a so-called limited war, for example across the territory of Western Europe, could be appalling'; and, in any case, 'the size of East/West nuclear armouries and the means available to deliver them are such that whatever the course of any limited engagement with nuclear weapons, the side temporarily coming off worst would always have a powerful alternative to defeat – the alternative of raising the stakes, of escalation' (p. 143). Although he concedes that this is an alternative, he does not believe that it is a very likely one:

Escalation is not an inexorable scientific process; it is a matter of human decision, to be taken moreover in circumstances of which we have fortunately no fully comparable past experience. We do not know, and I hope we never find out, precisely how statesmen – or soldiers, for that matter – will react if these fearful weapons ever start to fly about. Anyone, however eminent, who tells us that escalation is a certainty, or who purports to put a tidy figure of percentage probability upon it, is talking through his hat. The reality is surely this. No aggressor could afford to bring down thousands of nuclear weapons on his homeland. If he attacks, therefore, it must have been on a calculation that the defender would lack the resolve to use the weapons. There must be at least some possibility that when met by a nuclear response, even on a comparatively modest scale, he may re-assess his earlier calculation, and prefer to back off rather than take the risks of going on. NATO's policy in the field of theatre nuclear weapons is based on maximizing that possibility, be it large or small (pp. 143f.).

But this defence of NATO policy ignores several crucial factors. It is left to General Beach, in his article, to point out some of these:

Would escalation occur? Again there can be no certainty. It is a fair point that in circumstances where the Russians were deliberate aggressors, with the possession of Western Europe their desired prize, it could not conceivably be in their interest to devastate it nor could the cost ever be worth while. But this argument overlooks certain vital points. First the Russians have plainly said, and it is intrinsic to their doctrine, that any use of NATO of nuclear weapons in Europe will be met by massive retaliation in kind. Secondly, rather than as a deliberately planned act of annexation, war in Europe might arise much more untidily and ambiguously – perhaps as a result of recurring and worsening instability within Eastern Europe. Thirdly, if the alternative in Soviet eyes were outright defeat, in such a dire conjunction the nuclear devastation of the adversary might indeed seem the lesser of evils (p. 127).

Of course, it is usually unwise to claim about something which has in fact never occurred that it is a 'certainty' or an 'inexorable scientific process'. Nevertheless, there do seem to be grounds for anxiety about nuclear escalation, even in the most limited use of nuclear weapons, between NATO and the Warsaw Pact. It is to his credit that Keith Ward recognizes this, even though, as I shall argue, it greatly damages the position he is attempting to defend. He points out that the likelihood of all-out nuclear war 'occurring does increase if one side in the conflict does not believe in flexible response, and if the other side seems to be prepared to use nuclear weapons to prevent even an overwhelming conventional attack (and that is the NATO doctrine of 'first use'). For that reason, the doctrines of first use and flexible response fail to solve the problem of the instability of the nuclear equation. For they make an actual use of nuclear weapons more likely; and, given the Russian attitude (even allowing for propaganda), that does make escalation to all-out nuclear war possible' (p. 64). Ward sees this as a reason for questioning NATO doctrine and, indeed, sees this doctrine as making 'the unjustifiable more likely, by however little' (p. 64). But apparently, he does not see it as a reason for believing that the use of *any* nuclear weapon is morally unjustifiable.

However, Ward is clear that participation in an all-out nuclear war is morally unjustifiable and in contravention of a just-war theory. So, he argues that what a just-war theory 'does not permit is the holding of an unlimited nuclear deterrent, where there is any likelihood of it being used. And it does not permit any longer a search for nuclear superiority which can only fuel an unending arms-race' (p. 65). Indeed, he is deeply suspicious of much present-day nuclear deterrence policy: 'the Americans at least used to have, and the Russians still have, a policy of releasing all their weapons at the earliest moment of a nuclear war. That is exactly the all-out war which is morally unjustifiable. And even as a form of deterrence, it is scarcely credible; for anyone would have to be mad to destroy the world' (p. 62). In this respect, as in a number of others, Ward differs significantly from several of the other contributors to *The Cross and the Bomb*.

There is much in Ward's article which might lead one to expect that he would be a critic of some of the other contributors. It has already been noted, in Chapter 2, that in contrast to others he maintains that the nuclear situation is inherently evil. He recognizes frankly that nuclear deterrence involves the threat, or apparent threat, 'however conditionally, to destroy millions of innocent people by massive nuclear attack' (p. 52). He sees that any nuclear attack 'will necessarily result in large numbers of innocent deaths, since nuclear weapons are inherently indiscriminate in their effects. In such a case, killing the innocent is not just a foreseen consequence of our action; it is a necessary part of the action itself' (p. 59). He continues: 'we are not just talking about some killing of private citizens who have the misfortune to live near missile silos. With the number of nuclear weapons in the world today, we are talking about the destruction of whole countries, of future generations by genetic mutation, of totally uninvolved countries by fall-out, of the structure of civilized life itself' (p. 59). In terms of the empirical facts about nuclear weapons set out in Chapter 1, Ward clearly recognizes the existence, destructiveness and expansion of present-day nuclear armoury. He also recognizes 'what is called "horizontal proliferation" – more countries developing a nuclear capability – as well as "vertical proliferation" – the constant attempt by nuclear-armed states to achieve a weapons superiority, by continued technological innovation and arms build-up. As a result of this process, we already have enough nuclear weapons in existence to destroy the world a number of times. But it follows that any use of such weapons by one of the super-powers – or, indeed, any form of war between them at all – could lead to an escalation to all-out nuclear war' (pp. 60f.).

So, Ward does seem to acknowledge all of the empirical features about nuclear weapons that I have argued are important. He sees them as destructive, expanding, proliferating and increasingly unstable. Further, he recognizes that the function of the nuclear weapons currently in existence is only ambiguously concerned with deterrence. He even admits that the use of *any* nuclear weapon in war could lead to all-out escalation and concludes with the observation that, 'there is a finite probability that any form of defence, by one major nuclear power against another, could lead to all-out nuclear war . . . we have a duty to defend, and a duty not to engage in all-out nuclear war; yet nuclear defence seems to put us on a course towards such a war' (p. 61).

Despite these conclusions, he does defend the notion of 'a balanced, limited nuclear deterrent':

> What we have to do is to threaten to cause a degree of damage to the enemy which will be unacceptable to him, against which he will have no defence, and which will be seen by him as a credible threat (one we may well carry out). If we have enough nuclear

weapons to destroy his major military installations and their adjacent territories, that does seem to be the minimum threat necessary to deter a nuclear first strike; and it is credible, in the sense that it could provide for the survival of our remaining peoples (p. 61).

He believes that such a notion does fall 'within the limits of the "Just War" theory, even if it is at the horrifying extremity of justifiability. I therefore think that it is unduly naive and simplistic to say that the possession or use of nuclear weapons could never be justified, in any conceivable circumstance' (p. 61). Unfortunately he does not follow through this claim with any clear demonstration that this notion of 'a balanced, limited nuclear deterrent' really is consonant with a just-war theory. He argues only as follows:

> It seems to me likely that the possession of nuclear weapons is such a strong deterrent that it makes any direct conflict between the super-powers and their client-states extremely improbable – and we must remember the appalling suffering and destruction any conventional war would cause, in the modern world. It thus decreases the likelihood of any war between the powers. However, if even a conventional war should occur, there is no point in pretending that countries with a capacity to make nuclear weapons might not then begin to do so. There is simply no way of banning nuclear weapons from the face of the earth. In that sense, there is no alternative to nuclear deterrence anyway. The monster has been unleashed; and we must discover ways to live with it (pp. 61f.).

In fact what this is, is a series of consequential justifications of the possession of nuclear weapons and not a demonstration that their use is consonant with a just-war theory. The following consequential justifications can be identified from this passage:

(*a*) the possession of nuclear weapons has the consequence of providing a strong deterrent;

(*b*) the destructive consequences of nuclear weapons must be offset by the destructive consequences of modern conventional weapons;

(*c*) the possession of nuclear weapons has the consequence of deterring the use of even conventional weapons in war;

(*d*) nuclear weapons should be maintained because others cannot be stopped from making them.

To these consequential arguments slightly earlier, he adds a fifth – one based upon the notion of nuclear blackmail:

> Suppose that we have an enemy with nuclear weapons. If we have none, he can quickly impose his will upon us by using them until we surrender, as we will have to sooner or later. That, after all, is how the United States terminated the war with Japan so quickly . . . I take this point to be quite decisive — without nuclear weapons, there is no defence against an aggressive enemy who has them (p. 60).

It is not my aim, at this stage, to return to a debate about consequential arguments, but simply to show that, whatever else he has done, he has not demonstrated that the use of nuclear weapons is ever consonant with a just-war theory. Indeed, if he had carefully examined the notion of 'a balanced, limited nuclear deterrent', and the possible use of the necessary weapons involved, in the light of a just-war theory, he might have concluded otherwise. Having already acknowledged so many daunting empirical facts about present-day nuclear weapons, his justification of nuclear deterrence should have been made doubly difficult.

Perhaps the clearest way to demonstrate this is to set out one of the Christian versions of the just-war theory and then to ask whether or not a use of the weapons necessary for 'a balanced, limited nuclear deterrent' might conform to its various clauses. The following version appears in a British Council of Churches publication:

> For a war to be 'just' it must
> (1) have been undertaken by a lawful authority;
> (2) have been undertaken for the vindication of an undoubted right that has been certainly infringed;
> (3) be a last resort, all peaceful means of settlement having failed;
> (4) offer the possibility of good to be achieved outweighing the evils that war would involve;

(5) be waged with a reasonable hope of victory for justice;

(6) be waged with right intention;

(7) use methods that are legitimate, i.e. in accordance with man's nature as a rational being, with Christian moral principles and international agreements.'[24]

(From T. R. Milford, ed., *The Valley of Decision,* BCC, 1961 – it was because it was concerned to examine the justifiability of nuclear weapons that this publication emphasized the final clause).

The use in war of any kind of nuclear weapon, even those involved in 'a balanced, limited nuclear deterrent', raises particular problems for clauses (4), (5) and (7) and possibly also for clauses (3) and (6).

The principle of proportionality contained in clause (4) is especially problematic in this context. Ward summarizes it (perhaps more appropriately) as the notion that 'the evil caused by war must be less than the evil it avoids' and argues that 'most people would agree that, if it was not possible to defend oneself successfully, or if the prosecution of war actually made the sustaining of a just society impossible, then the principle of proportion would be clearly contravened' (p. 59). And he does believe that this principle is contravened by all-out nuclear war. Such war is 'disproportionate to any conceivable end (except the end of national suicide, perhaps). A nuclear response could not prevent defeat. It can prevent victory; but only at the cost of the whole world. All-out nuclear war must consequently stand unequivocally condemned, under the principle of the "Just War" tradition. It is morally unjustifiable' (p. 60). But the difficulty is that he then concedes that the use of *any* nuclear weapon 'could lead to an escalation to all-out war' (p. 61). In the light of this, it is not at all clear how he thinks that those weapons involved in 'a balanced, limited nuclear deterrent' can avoid the same moral condemnation. It is only by insisting that weapons used in this limited context will not lead to nuclear escalation that one can avoid this.

Yet, supposing it could be shown that such weapons are not escalatory, there still remains a problem of proportion. The appalling destructiveness of any nuclear weapons should always raise doubts for Christians about whether their use in war could ever be judged to be less evil than the evil they seek to avoid. Many Christians still feel doubtful about whether the actual use of atomic bombs at Hiroshima and Nagasaki was consonant with this clause in just-war theory. It is quite wrong to pass moral judgment on those who fought in the last war and important to be conscious of those who 'helped to deliver many nations from what would in all probability have been a long period of subjugation to appalling evil' (*The Church and the Bomb,* p. 163). But if, in 1945, the long-term genetic repercussions (which are only now beginning to be understood in all their gravity), the indiscriminate killing of the innocent and the new possibilities of evil that it showed to the world, had been fully appreciated, these doubts might have been stronger at the time. Nor is this point softened by Quinlan's observation that 'it does seem to me very important to recognize that the ghastly events of August 1945 did not mean that war suddenly became nasty having previously been nice . . . I do remember the London Blitz' (p. 138). Some Christians have always felt (and in this they had the support of the emphatically non-pacifist William Temple) that mass civilian bombing is never consonant with a just-war theory. In any case, the atomic bombs used at Hiroshima and Nagasaki are hardly to be compared with the destructive weapons of today.

The principle of discrimination, contained in clauses (5) and (7), also raises problems for all uses of nuclear weapons in war. Ward describes this principle as the attempt 'to limit the number of people who may be the objects of violence in war. Force must be used with discrimination; it must be the minimum necessary; it must tend materially to the end of victory; and it should not involve the killing of the innocent' (pp. 56f.). Clearly, all-out nuclear war offends both of these clauses. In such a war there can be no reasonable hope of victory of any kind and the methods used to achieve such a situation can scarcely be described as 'legitimate', 'rational' or in accord with 'Christian moral principles'. Even the threat of such a war is seen by Ward as a threat 'to do the greater evil – since the destruction of the world is worse than the destruction of your own country' (pp. 62f.). If the notion of nuclear escalation is adopted, it is clear that the use of any nuclear weapon in war may produce a situation which contravenes the principle of discrimination. But, even if it is not adopted, it is difficult to see that the use of any single nuclear weapon could be seen by the Christian as 'legitimate', 'rational' and consonant with 'Christian moral principles'.

It probably follows from all of this that clause (6) is also contravened by any use of nuclear weapons. It might be held that the intentions of the Americans responsible for dropping the atomic bombs on Hiroshima and Nagasaki were 'right'. They did so because they believed (correctly) that this would bring the war to a swift end. They also believed that this, in itself, would save many lives (on both sides) which would have been lost in a protracted conflict and perhaps deter the Soviet or China from any similar conflict in the future. And finally, they may have been unaware of the long-term repercussions of using the bombs in this situation. But none of these consequential justifications is open today to potential users of nuclear weapons. The repercussions of using such weapons are now known and the weapons themselves are no longer the exclusive possessions of one military power. Anyone using these weapons today does so in the knowledge that they are appallingly destructive and widely available. They should also have at least the fear that their use might escalate into all-out nuclear war.

Clause (3) is one of the most troublesome for many types of war and is also one of the most frequently overlooked clauses in just-war theory. For the Christian who attempts to abide by a just-war theory, war is a last resort when 'all peaceful means of settlement have failed'. It is never legitimate, when negotiation is still possible, to use war as an alternative means of settling international disagreements. This is why the timing of the sinking of the *Belgrano,* at the start of the Falklands war, is so critical. If it can be shown that all peaceful means of settlement had not been exhausted before this action was taken, then it (and, of course, the prior Argentinian invasion of the islands) would appear to contravene a just-war theory. In the case of possible nuclear confrontations, it becomes even more vital that all peaceful means of settlement have been exhausted. More than that, it is arguable that peaceful means can never be sufficiently exhausted to make it permissible actually to release even limited nuclear weapons.

It is perhaps this clause which shows that the atomic bombing of Hiroshima and Nagasaki did contravene a just-war theory. In the circumstances, it would be very difficult now to show that all peaceful means (or, at the very least, all non-nuclear means) had been exhausted before two bombs were dropped. A clear and unambiguous demonstration of the appalling destruction that would follow the dropping of such bombs on cities might have been made without actually dropping them on cities. The Americans might have dropped a bomb, initially, on one of the many uninhabited Japanese islands together with the clear warning that, unless the enemy surrendered, a similar bomb would be dropped on a populated area. Arguing of course with the benefit of hindsight, it might seem that little would have been lost in time by doing this and much would have been gained in avoiding the subsequent horrors. If that had failed, then the bombing of a thinly populated part of Japan might have followed. And, if that had failed, then perhaps Hiroshima. But the bombing of both Hiroshima and Nagasaki within days, and at the very outset, is difficult to justify in terms of a Christian just-war theory. Doubtless feelings of war-weariness, and perhaps also revenge, outweighed such moral sentiments at the time, but these are not sufficient reasons for continuing to think that such actions are consonant with a just-war theory and morally permissible.

Of course there are problems in establishing and abiding by just-war theories.[25] In war-time itself, just-war principles tend to be constantly eroded as all sides become intent solely on victory. The mass bombings of Dresden and Coventry are clear examples of that. Further, it is difficult to establish clauses in such theories which will fit all possible situations. For example, clause (1) causes problems in revolutionary situations and in wars of 'liberation', in which it is far from clear who constitutes a 'lawful authority'. And, as will be seen in the next chapter, some Christians have always had problems in assessing the consistency of any justification of war with the New Testament.

None the less, Christian just-war theories, properly understood, are attempts to limit war and to persuade those of a Christian conscience to avoid unjustifiable wars and unjustifiable means of fighting within wars. At their best, as I argued at the end of Chapter 1, they express some of the reluctance and deep regret that Christians should feel about war and about the horrors of war. If, at times, the clauses of just-war theories have been converted into formalistic rules governing proper behaviour in battle, that was not the intention of those Christians who first adopted them. Ward is quite correct in arguing that just-war theories are attempts 'to minimize violence, both by restricting the numbers of people who may legitimately be the instruments and the objects of violence, and by placing limits on the kind or degree of violence that may be offered . . . A "just war" is one which meets these requirements. It is not, and has never been thought to be, a positively good thing. It is a use of well-regulated but violent force, a commission of evil, in order to prevent a greater evil' (p. 54). This was certainly Augustine's understanding of a 'just' war.

To claim that the use of nuclear weapons is never consonant with a just-war theory does not settle the nuclear issue. Nuclear weapons still exist and cannot be disinvented. As long as they exist, or even as long as the knowledge to make them and the means to manufacture them exist, they may be used in war. This possibility of use does not evaporate by demonstrating that, in terms of the traditional criteria which Christians have used to assess methods of war-fighting, they are unjustifiable. Nor does the possibility disappear that, if they consider that they have nothing to lose, those entirely untouched by Christian principles will have no moral scruples in using nuclear weapons in war. A realistic assessment of the present nuclear situation should not hesitate to acknowledge this. Only the most naive opinion could hold that mankind could first destroy and could then forget all about nuclear weapons. But what it does mean is that Christians have particular reason for proclaiming that the possession of nuclear weapons is evil and, for them, deeply sinful, and that in no circumstance can their use in war be justified.

5 *Is Nuclear Pacifism Morally Irresponsible?*

It is one of the most remarkable contrasts between the church until the late fourth century and the church ever since that while originally it was almost wholly pacifist, subsequently it has hardly ever been. [26] The church historian Roland Bainton argues that 'the age of persecution down to the time of Constantine was the age of pacifism to the degree that during this period no Christian author to our knowledge approved of Christian participation in battle' (*Christian Attitudes Toward War and Peace,* Abingdon Press 1960, p. 66). But today, thoroughgoing pacifism is confined to a minority of Christians within mainstream churches or denominations and to a minority of sects, such as the Amish Mennonites, Anabaptists, Brethren, Jehovah's Witnesses and Quakers. [27]

Even in the second century, there were a few individuals who were both Christians and soldiers, but almost certainly they were soldiers first who only later became Christians. Further, there were difficulties for Christians, in that being soldiers in the imperial army, they were associated with the 'pagan' ceremonies and sacrifices that surrounded it. But all the surviving early Christian writings, when they discuss warfare, defend a 'pacifist' position of one sort or another. Even though there are different types of pacifism evident within these writings, all *are* pacifist. Tertullian (*c.* 160-220) tended, especially in later life, to be absolutist in his rejection of human killing of any kind:

> Moses carried a rod, and Aaron wore a buckle, and John (Baptist) is girt with leather, and Joshua the son of Nun leads a line of march; and the people warred: if it please you to sport the subject. But how will a Christian man war, nay, how will he serve even in peace, without a sword, which the Lord has taken away?

For albeit soldiers had come unto John, and had received the formula of their rule; albeit, likewise, a centurion had believed; still the Lord afterward, in disarming Peter, unbelted every soldier' (*On Idolatry* 19, from *The Ante-Nicene Fathers,* Vol. 3).

Thus, Tertullian was fully aware of the Old Testament sanction of war and even of Jesus' contacts with soldiers, but believed that the admonition of Peter at Gethsemane finally prohibited Christians from using weapons of war.

Origen (*c.* 185-254) also believed that Jesus forbade altogether 'the putting of men to death' and 'nowhere teaches that it is right for his own disciples to offer violence to anyone, however wicked' (*Against Celsus* 3.7). Nevertheless, his pacifism tended to be more pragmatic than that of Tertullian. He was determined to refute the charge, which had been made against Christians, that their pacifism was responsible for undermining the state. To counter this, he argued that although Christians cannot become soldiers, they can be of even greater use by fighting with their prayers:

> To those enemies of our faith who require us to bear arms for the commonwealth, and to slay men, we can reply: 'Do not those who are priests at certain shrines, and those who attend on certain gods, as you account them, keep their hands free from blood, that they may with their hands unstained and free from human blood offer the appointed sacrifices to your gods; and even when war is upon you, you never enlist the priests in the army. If that, then, is a laudable custom, how much more so, that while others are engaged in battle, these should engage as the priests and ministers of God, keeping their hands pure, and wrestling in prayers to God on behalf of those who are fighting in a righteous cause, and for the king who reigns righteously, that whatsoever is opposed to those who act righteously may be destroyed!' (*Against Celsus* 8.73).

With Augustine (354-430),[28] living at a time when Christianity had been adopted as the 'state religion', there is evident a radical shift of attitude towards Christian participation in war. Like Origen, he too was concerned to counter pagan critics and to insist that rulers who wage war can do so 'righteously'. But, unlike Origen and Tertullian, he believed that Christians could properly be soldiers, indeed, that if called upon to do so by a lawful authority, Christians, along with other citizens, had a duty to fight. He came to see the sanction of war in the Old Testament as confirmation of this position. Turning to the New Testament, he offered a radically different interpretation to that of Tertullian. Referring to the same incident at Gethsemane, he argued:

> To take the sword is to use weapons against a man's life, without the sanction of the constituted authority. The Lord, indeed, had told his disciples to carry a sword; but he did not tell them to use it. But that after this sin Peter should become a pastor of the church was no more improper than that Moses, after smiting the Egyptian, should become the leader of the congregation. In both cases the trespass originated not in inveterate cruelty, but in hasty zeal which admitted of correction. In both cases there was resentment against injury, accompanied in one case by love for a brother, and in the other by love, though still carnal, of the Lord (*Reply to Faustus the Manichaean* XXII 69f, from *The Nicene and Post-Nicene Fathers,* Vol. 4).

So, Peter was really guilty of 'hasty zeal'. More to the point, in Augustine's analysis, he acted violently without 'lawful authority': he acted without the authority either of the state or of God himself.

With Aquinas[29] (*c.*1225-74) the process became complete. He fully accepted Augustine's concept of the 'just war' and believed that any violence, if it is to be justified, must be undertaken only on 'lawful authority'. So it is permissible to kill in the context of a 'just' war or even to practise capital punishment. But it is not permissible for the individual to act violently without such authority. Further, he understood the Gethsemane incident as referring to the clergy alone: 'The words, "Put your sword back in its scabbard" were directed to Peter as representing all bishops and clerics. Consequently, they may not fight' (*Summa Theologica,* 2a2ae.40.2, English Dominican translation). By this rather strange route there became established the clerical injunction against their own active participation in warfare.

It is difficult to avoid the conclusion that, at least in part, this radical shift in Christian attitudes resulted from a change of political status.[30] With the adoption of Christianity by Constantine as a state religion, the role of Christians in society inevitably changed. They were forced to take seriously the problems inherent in running a nation and, indeed, an empire. Whereas formerly they could espouse pacifism, now they tended to view society from the perspective of those who were attempting to govern it. Augustine, in old age, even went so far as to enlist the help of the military to suppress a group of Christians that he regarded as 'heretics', the Donatists, and combined the roles of bishop and magistrate. And, today, it is precisely those minority Christian movements that tend to reject society at large which are most likely to espouse Tertullian's absolutist pacifism. Modern Quakers, who frequently occupy important roles in society, lean rather to Origen's pragmatic and exemplary pacifism.[31] Mainstream churches and denominations, on the other hand, have a strong tendency to reject pacifism altogether.

However understandable, this radical shift has caused serious problems for Christianity. It was obvious to the young Augustine that, on such issues as war, there was a dichotomy between the Old Testament and the New. For some years this prevented him from becoming a Christian, and only with considerable difficulty did he ever resolve the dichotomy. He was forced to reverse the judgments on New Testament pacifism of his fellow North African, Tertullian, and borrowed considerably from the classical thought in which he had been trained – not least in his notions of a 'just war'. He tended to stress passages in the New Testament, such as Romans 13, which emphasized the importance of obedience to rulers, and was one of the first to introduce arguments from silence about Jesus' own attitudes to war and the 'Roman peace' ensured by the Roman military. And he frequently used the Old Testament as a guide to Christian conduct and defended seemingly 'unjust' incidents of war and violence within it as being products of God's direct command.

Some of these processes have already been observed in the contributions to *The Cross and the Bomb*. A recognition of 'authority' is seen by Graham Leonard as a key element of both Old and New Testaments:

> In the Old Testament the authority and power of Cyrus, King of Persia, was, for example, used by God in the preparation of the people of Israel for the coming of Christ; in the New Testament the authority of Caesar is recognized both by Our Lord and in the Epistles. St Paul makes it clear in Romans 13 that one of its functions is to witness to the distinction between good and evil and to help man to be true to his moral nature. The readers of 1 Peter are told to use the freedom which government provides as bondservants of God and not for a cloak of wickedness. The recognition and acceptance of authority carries with it recognition and acceptance of the power which is its ultimate sanction (pp. 6f.).

And Richard Harries provides a revealing illustration of a present-day argument from silence about Jesus' attitude towards war:

> The position taken here is that Jesus did think that the kingdom, the decisive rule of God in human affairs, was near and that his ethical teaching has to be seen in integral relationship to that conviction. In other words if he had believed that human society would continue in its old way for thousands of years he would have balanced his teaching by more emphasis on what he took for granted, namely the law of the Old Testament. The law of the Old Testament is applicable to the management of human society. Jesus assumes this (p. 83).

The difficulty is that this presumes to know, not only what Jesus assumed but never actually mentioned, but even what Jesus would have said had he not been mistaken about the life-expectancy of human society. It does not stop with what is more evident – that Jesus passed no direct judgment about human warfare, but did make frequent mention of forgiving enemies and himself offered no violence to his own persecutors.[32] It was precisely this which was most evident to the early church and even to some of Christianity's earliest opponents.

Ulrich Simon, Professor Emeritus of Christian Literature at

King's College, London, best expresses some of the tension in the earliest church on the issue of war and violence:

> The Apostolic Church lives by this Gospel which modern analysts may well call a dialectical attitude to life. On the one hand the chosen band of disciples forswears violence and is not touched by military and political events, shows its loyalty to the powers that be by paying tribute and by dissociating itself from revolutionary armed activity; on the other the missionary activity, first in Judaea, then in Samaria, and soon in the Greek speaking world, until even Rome is reached, proclaims Christ as a way of life, as an abolition of the old and the fulfilment of the new. Neither Peter nor Paul nor the ordinary Christians strike us as 'lambs', in the sense in which Nietzsche and his followers understood and loathed the religion of the pale Nazarene (p. 104).

Simon argues that I Peter offers the 'subtlest presentation of the paradox' in the earliest church. In a description of I Peter, in startling contrast to that offered by Leonard, he writes:

> One wonders how the writer and the recipients, whom we cannot locate with any certainty, envisage their daily lamb-like existence in the empire. They acknowledge the power of emperor and magistrate, of law and order, even if oppressive; they would carry on their perfectionist lives in subjection to this order because they acknowledge God as the sole author of cosmic life and government. The most radical view is taken of martyrdom as a Christ-like witness not only to good but also to wicked powers. The tone of the exhortation is to the community, but individuals are expected to heed the counsel of perfection. The context is still eschatological. Hence the demonic onslaughts can be endured because the end is in sight. This end is not death but eternal life. Just as the slaughtered Lamb is enthroned as the shepherd of souls so the souls of the martyrs will be transformed into his likeness (pp. 104f.).

In the next chapter, I shall argue that for Christians in a nuclear, apocalyptic age, a return to some of these paradoxical attitudes is vital. For the moment, it is important to note that little of the paradox characterizes the main contributors to *The Cross and the Bomb* in their concern to defend nuclear deterrence.

Indeed, throughout the book there is a strong polemic running against pacifism of any description. Even Simon begins his article with the uncompromising claim that 'pacifists differ in kind but have an identical aim, namely to achieve peace by peaceful means. Even in the nuclear age they envisage nuclear free zones and are prepared to work towards total disarmament unilaterally. Such a policy implies a submission to a power or powers which contemplate no similar action . . . The unarmed will be taken over by the armed' (p. 93). And throughout his article he tends to regard pacifists as simply those who offer no resistance to evil whatsoever, as exponents of what he terms 'Christian Buddhism' (p. 106). Leonard acccepts pacifism as a legitimate vocation for individual Christians. He maintains that 'I fully accept that there are those who believe that they have a vocation to embrace this position and must in conscience do so. I respect them and I believe that they have a significant role to play in the world not unlike that played by monks or nuns in the Christian Church' (p. 13). As he has already defined pacifism as the 'view which denies the right ever to take up arms even if one's country or oneself is threatened with subjugation or extinction' (p. 13) this conclusion is hardly surprising. Since, in the position channelled through Aquinas, clergy are prohibited from bearing arms even in self-defence, in this sense they are all pacifists. None the less, Leonard finds 'great difficulty when pacifism is advocated as a policy which should be adopted by those who have the responsibility of government' (p. 13). Again, in a democratic society, it is difficult to see that politicians can disarm those they govern unless the latter themselves have renounced arms. But his argument goes further. He maintains that 'pacifism does not bring peace either in the sense of absence of conflict or of harmony' and is thus 'a misnomer' (p. 14). Pacifism even 'elevates the moral demand not to take up arms in such a way that other moral demands, such as those presented by justice or truth, have not merely to take second place but have no place at all' (p. 14).

In order to show that pacifism is essentially naive and irresponsible in several of the articles this polemic against it is accompanied by examples taken from the behaviour of individuals. Previous chapters have noted this tendency so often already that it is unnecessary to cite again all the instances of it in *The Cross and the Bomb*. Those familiar with arguments against pacifism will recognize the mode of argument – e.g. what pacifist would not shoot an intruder who was about to rape his wife and murder his children? Indeed, Leonard states that he has not 'met a pacifist who declines to take advantage of the police force, who is not content to benefit from the conditions provided by his local authority, or who objects to calling upon the courts in any matter' (pp. 7f.). It is, perhaps, surprising to find such arguments in a serious discussion of Christian ethics. Such versions of the individualistic fallacy ignore the obvious point that pacifism is essentially an attitude towards war and not towards acts of individual violence. The division between Christian pacifists and Christian just-war theorists is not a division about the legitimacy of individually inspired acts of violence. It is about whether or not a 'lawful authority' can legitimately require individuals to kill in the context of war, and about whether individuals should then feel themselves obliged to do so.

This point becomes apparent if one attempts to distinguish between the various options that are open to individuals responding to a requirement to fight in war. In *Theology and Social Structure* (Mowbrays 1977, p. 71) I suggested the following four general types of response:

(a) *Thoroughgoing Militarism:* understood as a willingness to fight anywhere, at any time and for any cause.

(b) *Selective Militarism:* understood as a willingness to fight when one's country, or another, declares that the cause is just.

(c) *Selective Pacifism:* understood as a willingness to fight only when one is convinced that the cause is just.

(d) *Thoroughgoing Pacifism:* understood as an unwillingness to fight anywhere, at any time and for any cause.

Of course there are various positions between these four general types and, in practice, individuals may show evidence, at different moments, of more than one type. But together they demonstrate the spectrum of possible positions.

Few would consider type (*a*) a Christian response. The non-idealistic mercenary would be an obvious example of this type. Curiously, Luther was one of the very few theologians to justify the role of the mercenary, arguing that 'a craftsman may sell his skill to anyone who will have it, and thus serve the one to whom he sells, so long as this is not against his ruler and his community. In the same way a soldier has his skill in fighting from God and can use it in the service of whoever desires to have it, exactly as though his skill were an art or trade, and he can take pay for it as he would for his work' (*Whether Soldiers, too, Can be Saved* [1526], in *Luther's Works,* Fortress Press, Vol. 46, p. 132). But even he did not justify the role of the mercenary anywhere, at any time and for any cause.

Of the other three types, (*b*) and (*c*) both presuppose some way of distinguishing between 'just' and 'unjust' causes. For Christians, both depend upon a just-war tradition, applied either by, or on behalf of, the individual concerned. On the other hand, type (*d*) represents the kind of pacifism evident in some of Tertullian's writings and characteristic of a number of pacifist sects today. All three types are essentially concerned with *moral responses to war* and not with the legitimacy of individually inspired violence or even with police coercion within a society.

It should also be evident that, for the vast majority of people, these four types have little relevance to the nuclear situation. In conventional war, the individual is required by his country to fight and it is for the individual, as a person of conscience, to decide whether or not to respond to this requirement. But in nuclear war, even in a limited war involving the use of short-range nuclear weapons, only a tiny group of professional soldiers will actually be involved in fighting. Others may protest or applaud (or, more likely, simply die) but there can be no question of their personal involvement in the actual nuclear exchanges. In this sense, for all but a very few, the whole debate about pacifism and non-pacifism is an anachronistic debate. Whatever else it is, 'nuclear pacifism' is not pacifism in any traditional sense.

Yet the contributors to *The Cross and the Bomb* frequently

assume that 'nuclear pacifism' *is* a form of 'pacifism' and that, if the latter can be shown to be naive and irresponsible, then 'nuclear pacifism' too must be naive and irresponsible. So, Leonard argues that 'a particular form of pacifism has emerged which can be described as nuclear pacifism, that is the view that while it is possible to acquiesce in the use of conventional weapons, horrific though they are, nuclear weapons are so evil and have such evil consequences that they must be abandoned at all costs. This view shares all the difficulties presented by traditional pacifism for if any form of force is accepted, it is that which presents the ultimate sanction which really matters. Even if attempts were made to restrict war to the use of conventional weapons, nuclear weapons or their possibility would always remain and could always be used for blackmail' (p. 14). Indeed, this is another obvious difference between 'nuclear pacifism' and any other form of pacifism. In most instances 'nuclear pacifism' is a form of protest, protest knowing that that which is protested against can never be disinvented.

Pacifism aside, it might still be claimed that unilateralism is naive and irresponsible. Even if one concedes some of the empirical ambiguities surrounding nuclear 'deterrence' (as discussed in Chapter 1), it might still be claimed that it would be morally irresponsible to abandon precipitately one's own nuclear weapons and thus to put at risk the current nuclear balance. So, arguing from an intrinsic perspective, even though the possession of nuclear weapons is evil and their use in war unjustifiable, their precipitate disposal would be even more evil. Similarly, arguing now from a consequential perspective, the consequences of precipitately abandoning present-day nuclear weapons would be more dangerous and thus more evil than the consequences of maintaining the current nuclear balance (quite regardless of whether the latter does or does not constitute a deterrent).

Put like this, these arguments avoid most of the weaknesses that have been criticized up to this point. They do not depend upon a theory of deterrence, but rather upon a notion of nuclear balance. They do not underestimate the danger of nuclear weapons. Indeed, it is their very dangerousness which counsels caution and the avoidance of precipitate action. They do not seek to justify directly the possession or use of nuclear weapons, but rather to criticize their precipitate abandonment. They do not even deny that maintaining nuclear weapons (which are fast expanding and proliferating) has dangerous consequences. They simply point to the moral irresponsibility of creating a situation in which the use of nuclear weapons in war might become more likely. In an area fraught with such danger and yet lacking serious precedents, all thinking people should take this warning to heart.

The authors of the Anglican report *The Church and the Bomb* are certainly well aware of this danger. In discussing unilateralism they declare at the outset:

> Total abandonment of nuclear weapons by one of the alliances in the international line-up could undoubtedly have serious destabilizing effects. As a policy option, however, it lies in the realm of fantasy as things are at present (p. 134).

This Report quotes, with approval, a British Council of Churches' statement drawing attention to 'the importance of carrying out unilateral acts in a way that would increase the chance that they would be reciprocated, thus improving the international climate, and starting a process of building confidence and trust' (*The Church and the Bomb,* p. 133). In this the Report is following Charles Osgood's eight guidelines for responsible unilateralism:

(i) Each unilateral step must be perceived by the opponent as reducing the external threat to him. (It is no good, e.g., simply phasing out obsolete missiles.)

(ii) Each unilateral step should be accompanied by an explicit invitation to reciprocate.

(iii) Unilateral acts should be undertaken whether or not an adversary makes a prior commitment to reciprocate.

(iv) Unilateral acts should be planned in sequence and persisted in over substantial periods of time, whether or not an opponent openly reciprocates.

(v) Each step should be announced before it is taken, and given full publicity.

(vi) Whenever possible, initiatives should concentrate on areas of mutual interest and opportunities for co-operation.

(vii) Steps should be graduated in risk so as to avoid undue dangers during the early period.

(viii) Unilateral initiatives should be accompanied by firmness towards the adversary (p. 133: from Charles Osgood, *An Alternative to War or Surrender,* University of Illinois Press, 1962).

Whatever else it might be, clearly this is not a blueprint for precipitate action. Following these guidelines, unilateral disarmament would not involve a precipitate abandonment of nuclear weapons. Such abandonment would be gradual, phased and carefully designed to evoke corresponding action in others. Further, the authors of the Report are aware that such action would not in itself resolve the problems of modern warfare:

> If nuclear weapons were abandoned universally tomorrow, behind them stand the further spectres of chemical and biological warfare; and, as has been said many times, the nuclear weapons themselves cannot be disinvented – their possibility is with us for ever. Humanity cannot come to some agreement on nuclear weapons and lapse back into the old attitudes. The task of nuclear disarmament is only the first and most urgent instalment of the major political, social, educational, psychological and religious undertaking of eradicating war altogether from the world's agenda (*The Church and the Bomb,* p. 163).

The specific unilateral acts the authors of the Report support are intended to be 'strategies which care about security and stability, but which will also break the log-jam in which we seem to be caught . . . in the hope of getting multilateral reductions moving . . . The aim of negotiation, we believe, should be to arrive *in the end* at much lower and balanced force levels in every category of weapons (eventually, of course, balancing at nil), not necessarily to achieve equality at every stage' (*The Church and the Bomb,* p. 159). On this basis they propose:

The United Kingdom should renounce its independent nuclear deterrent. We make this recommendation for two reasons; first, in the hope of putting new life into the Non-Proliferation Treaty, by showing that at least one of the nuclear powers is prepared to take its obligations under this instrument seriously; second, to eliminate what we feel to be a destabilising element in the world situation, Britain's ambiguously separate centre of decision making on the use of nuclear weapons (*The Church and the Bomb*, p. 160).

They believe that this should be achieved by cancelling the Trident missile at once and by phasing out the Polaris missiles. Then Britain should withdraw, first from British-made nuclear weapons, then from US-made depth bombs, missiles and artillery, under dual key control, and finally from US air and submarine base facilities. The timetable for implementing these withdrawals would be 'a matter for negotiation with Britain's allies, but the decision to undertake the whole process should be taken in the same single political operation' – as, indeed, the Osgood guidelines propose (*The Church and the Bomb*, p. 160).

Despite his own reservations about the deterrent function of Britain's independent nuclear weapons (which I have already set out in Chapter 1), Hugh Beach is not convinced by these recommendations:

The truth is that the authors of *The Church and the Bomb* seek nuclear disarmament for its own sake, in pursuit of what they believe to be the Christian decision. Dodging the logic they seek to apply this precept to Britain, and Britain alone, because to do so more widely would be – as they accurately perceive – highly dangerous. The concept of making renunciation 'a unilateral step within a multilateral process' is dragged in as an afterthought. If one were to begin with this objective then the point would be quite obvious that the best way to promote multilateral negotiations is precisely to take part in them – in as hard headed a way as is possible – and with the aim of securing as rapid and far-reaching results as possible within the realms of prudence. This in itself will require reduction in Britain's nuclear stance – probably the abrogation of complete capabilities – but always in concert with allies as to the principle as well as to timing and to consequentials. Here is a cause for the Christian Churches, in all the countries, to pursue with honesty, clear sightedness, logic and the pragmatism which is the report's strongest point. That then becomes a duty (*The Cross and the Bomb,* pp. 131f.).

This is an extremely important and constructive proposal. And it is certainly not for the theologian to pretend that he or she knows how military/political negotiations should be most effectively conducted. None the less, as Beach himself is well aware, at present there are difficulties in implementing such a proposal. International multilateral negotiations keep on reaching an impasse and it is precisely in order to break this impasse that the Anglican Report is proposing some unilateral act on the part of Britain. Further, Britain has not taken part officially in the negotiations – SALT, START and INF – which have been conducted to date. Beach argues that 'there is no logic in their exclusion from the intermediate nuclear force negotiations, and the USSR has pressed, from the beginning, for their inclusion . . . the principle of including the British forces in these negotiations, though stoutly resisted by British officials, is beyond all question logical' (pp. 118f.). This is a very significant criticism, but it does highlight the empirical difficulties facing his proposal.

But would a unilateral act on the part of Britain really break the impasse faced by multilateral negotiations? This, too, is an empirical question and one that theology provides no special expertise to answer. Beach is sceptical and believes that this unilateral proposal 'represents a triumph of hope over experience. The overwhelming likelihood is that other nations will continue to do what they always have done, and that is to take their decision of high policy on the basis of what they consider to be their own national interest. The notion that they would be shamed into following us is sentimental not to say sanctimonious. Historical precedents tell in exactly the other direction – chemical warfare being a case in point. The UK renounced an offensive capability 25 years ago, and since then has seen the Soviet offensive capability more than double. Gesture having proved wholly inappropriate to this type of issue, it is plain that there is no substitute for hard bargaining (p. 118). [33]

There is obvious common sense in this argument. Reinhold Niebuhr might have been used, once more, to reinforce the point that it is fallacious to apply individual moral categories to social issues. Even if individuals can be influenced by 'moral gestures', nations are far more likely to be guided by self-interest. But it could be argued that it *is* in the long-term self-interest of nations to control arms and to limit drastically nuclear weapons. It is certainly in their immediate self-interest to halt the expansion and proliferation of nuclear weapons. Viewed in this way, unilateralism would be less of a moral gesture than of an initial demonstration of what is in the interest of all to achieve. Rather than as a substitute for hard bargaining, it would be intended as a prelude to it.

All of these arguments, for and against unilateralism, are consequential arguments. By implication, Beach is critical of intrinsic arguments in this context, of arguments for 'nuclear disarmament for its own sake', and commends the Anglican Report for its 'pragmatism'. In contrast, Keith Ward argues primarily from an intrinsic perspective. Having concluded that all-out nuclear warfare and a deterrent which threatens such warfare are unjustifiable, he argues:

It is therefore imperative to dismantle the apparatus which makes all-out war possible, and to cease relying on the threat to resort to it. If we must live with the monster of nuclear weaponry, we must at least cage it securely. But how is this to be done? In a situation where each super-power can destroy the other, it seems that the minimum that sanity requires is a Comprehensive Test Ban Treaty; an end to further development of nuclear weapons which could be seen as offensive; an end to the impossible search for 'parity' of nuclear weapons; an end to reliance on the first use of nuclear weapons to counter conventional attack; and the beginning of deep cuts in the stockpiles of the super-powers (pp. 64f.).

He proceeds to attack the concept of nuclear parity (which Harries subsequently defends) and to argue that 'we can encourage both Russia and America to make unilateral cuts, if necessary, since it will have no effect on their deterrent capacity. In other words, we can concentrate on strengthening our conventional defence, and hold our particular forces well back, at a limited level, and solely for the purpose of discouraging a nuclear attack upon us by threatening an unacceptably damaging response' (p. 65). He sees this as a necessary stage to 'a much more complete nuclear disarmament. But that must be a mutual process. It is in this sense that I am a "multilateralist" ' (p. 65). But, of course, everyone should be a multilateralist in this sense. Indeed, from his conclusions, it is puzzling that Ward is a critic of the Anglican Report at all – especially since he concludes that 'there are steps that can be taken now, both to start the multilateral process going by a clear renunciation of the goal of nuclear parity at every level; and to stabilize the deterrence equation by decreasing the scale of destruction a retaliatory nuclear strike would cause. I believe that when the arguments are set out clearly, a moral obligation emerges to act at once, and without conditions, to make all-out (unlimited) nuclear war impossible' (pp. 65f.).

Returning to Beach, it is one thing to recognize frankly that countries act basically out of self-interest, but it is quite another for Christians to acquiesce in their own country acting *only* out of self-interest. If, through careful moral scrutiny, it becomes evident to Christians that the possession of nuclear weapons is wrong and unjustifiable, then they cannot be content solely with arguments about national self-interest. [34] If moral propriety cannot always be the chief concern in international negotiations, it ought not to be considered as simply irrelevant to them. Even at the most pragmatic level, a combination of moral repugnance at nuclear weapons and long-term national self-interest for strict control might seem more powerful than short-term self-interest alone. This combinaton is present in the final paragraph of the Anglican Report:

> If we persist in pinning our hopes on nuclear weapons we are simply gambling with the lives and well being of the innocent and

the unborn. No considerations whatever can give us the right to do this. We are convinced that for this country to take a positive and courageous stand on this issue would do miracles for the moral vitality and temper of our national life . . . (*The Church and the Bomb,* p. 164).

6 *Christians in a Nuclear World*

So far I have attempted to scrutinize four of the claims made in *The Cross and the Bomb* – that nuclear deterrence is not wrong in itself; that nuclear deterrence is not wrong in its consequences; that the use of certain nuclear weapons can be justified in terms of a Christian just-war theory; and that unilateralism and 'nuclear pacifism' are morally irresponsible and, perhaps, even evil. These claims are not made consistently by the various authors and at several crucial points divergences between them have been noted. None the less, taken together, they amount to a strong moral justification of the possession of nuclear weapons.

The importance of this justification becomes apparent once it is seen that there has been a growing ecumenical consensus on the nuclear issue and an increasing tendency for Christian ethicists to regard the possession of nuclear weapons as morally dubious. Whilst some still maintain that 'possession' and 'use' pose quite separate moral difficulties, many insist that, at least in the nuclear context, possession implies an intention to use if this proves necessary. Even a notion of nuclear deterrence based upon bluff requires the overwhelming majority of those involved to be so intent. In any case, some of the contributors to *The Cross and the Bomb* are prepared to justify uses of nuclear weapons in war, albeit limited uses. All of this is in marked contrast to the growing unease of other Christian ethicists and church leaders.

Both Pope Pius XII and Pope Paul VI at times expressed unease about whether nuclear weapons really were consistent with traditional just-war notions of discrimination and proportionality. And the Vatican II document *Gaudium et Spes* argued significantly:

The development of armaments by modern science has

immeasurably magnified the horrors and wickedness of war.
Warfare conducted with these weapons can inflict immense and
indiscriminate havoc which goes far beyond the bounds of
legitimate defence . . . All these factors force us to undertake a
completely fresh re-appraisal of war. Men of this generation
should realize that they will have to render an account of their
warlike behaviour; the destiny of generations to come depends
largely on the decisions they make today. With these
considerations in mind the Council, endorsing the
condemnations of total warfare issued by recent popes, declares:
Every act of war directed to the indiscriminate destruction of
whole cities or vast areas with their inhabitants is a crime against
God and man, which merits firm and unequivocal
condemnation (para. 80).

The document also strongly agreed with Pope John XXIII's
contention that, 'in this age of ours, which prides itself on its atomic
power, it is irrational to think that war is a proper way to obtain
justice for violated rights' (*Pacem in Terris* 127).

The World Council of Churches, whilst reluctantly accepting
nuclear deterrence as a temporary measure, argued that 'the
production and deployment as well as the use of nuclear weapons
are a crime against humanity' (27 July 1982 – see also the report of
the Amsterdam hearings, *Before It Is Too Late,* WCC 1983). This is
very close to Pope John Paul II's claim that 'in current conditions
"deterrence" based on balance, certainly not as an end in itself but
as a step on the way towards a progressive disarmament, may still be
judged morally acceptable. None the less, in order to ensure peace,
it is indispensable not to be satisfied with this minimum which is
always susceptible to the real danger of explosion' (Message to UN
Special Session on Disarmament, n. 8, 11 June 1982). Even more
emphatically, British RC Bishops declared:

We re-affirm the declaration that we made in 1978 calling on Her
Majesty's Government to engage in negotiations designed to
produce an international agreement to bring about the total
elimination of nuclear weapons. We repeat what we said in *The
Easter People* that 'we are deeply concerned about the morality

involved in the possession of the nuclear deterrent'. We are agreed that it is never legitimate to use a weapon of indiscriminate mass destruction against the inhabitants of whole cities or vast areas [35] (Statement from the Bishops' Conference of England and Wales, Nov. 1980).

These moral reservations about the possession of nuclear weapons have, at times, expressed themselves in terms of explicit commitments to forms of unilateralism by the Assemblies of both the British Council of Churches (see *On Making Peace in a Nuclear World,* BCC 1983) and a number of Reformed Churches, including the Church of Scotland and the British Methodist Church (see the report of the Division of Social Responsibility, *Nuclear Disarmament: Some Theological Considerations,* accepted by the Methodist Conference, June 1983). It is clear that the position adopted by the authors of the Anglican report, *The Church and the Bomb,* is by no means exceptional.

In contrast, the claims of *The Cross and the Bomb* seek to justify the present-day possession of nuclear weapons, albeit with reservations by some of the contributors, and to present a Christian case for multilateralism. I believe that they are wrong. I have argued that the possession of nuclear weapons *is* inherently evil and, indeed, sinful; that the deterrent function of nuclear weapons is doubtful and that their possession cannot be adequately justified in consequence; that the use of nuclear weapons in war is incompatible with a Christian just-war theory and, in these terms, is unjustifiable; and, that unilateralism need not be irresponsible if it abides by strict guidelines, avoids precipitate action and has as its eventual goal multilateral negotiation and weapons reduction. Further, the fact that I have been at such pains to contest the claims of *The Cross and the Bomb,* suggests that I find them deeply disturbing. In particular, I find it disturbing that such an influential group of theologians should be seen to occupy a public role in legitimating the possession and potential use of such deeply sinful weapons.

Inevitably, all of this is negative and critical. What more can be done by Christians in a nuclear age? Fr Roger Ruston, OP, asks the same question at the end of a discussion in which he, too, concludes that the possession of present-day nuclear weapons cannot be justified in Christian terms. In a postscript, entitled 'Getting Out of Nuclear Deterrence', he writes:

Is it the case that we are attempting to defend ourselves with immoral threats which run counter to the Christian tradition concerning peace and the sanctity of life? That is the question we have to decide first. There would seem to be adequate grounds for deciding this. What we must not say is that, because it appears to be extremely difficult to escape from nuclear deterrence once we have entered into it, we are morally justified in continuing with it, until we can find something better. This attitude – which sometimes presents itself as a kind of 'Christian realism' – is in fact very close to fatalism. We must recognise that 'the world as it is' is a product of the things we are doing; overwhelmingly in 1982, the steadfast pursuance of the illusory security of the arms race and the balance of terror. We are threatening other countries with annihilation in the event of their committing aggression against us or our allies. Our potential enemies are doing the same to us. We must not say that we are compelled to continue with what we are doing. We must not say that the realistic Christian must make the best of a bad job, when the 'bad job' gets worse all the time we do it. To take a specific example, it is often said that nuclear weapons cannot be disinvented. This is obviously true and it has, of course, changed everything. But what we are faced with is not merely something invented in 1945, but the *continuous invention* of more and more sophisticated types of nuclear weapons. All these are the products of government policies and financing, scientific teamwork, military demands, etc., just as the first invention was. It is not natural necessity but human intentions which are the cause of it. And these can be changed (*Nuclear Deterrence – Right or Wrong?,* prepared for the Commission for International Justice and Peace of England and Wales, Catholic Information Services 1981, p. 67).

Here, indeed, is something that Christians can seek to do –

change human attitudes and intentions. But to do this, they must first be convinced that the possession of nuclear weapons is inherently evil and that their use as deterrents in peace and as weapons in war, is unjustifiable. If Christians are not themselves convinced of this, they should not expect to change the attitudes and intentions of others. If they are seen by others to be rather legitimating the possession of nuclear weapons, they can expect no change at all. Conviction about the sinfulness of the present-day nuclear situation is important to change attitudes. But it is not sufficient. Action is also required: social and political action.

Perhaps the differing options on the nuclear issue confronting Christians today can be seen more clearly by examining a social issue that was of central concern to Christians in the last century. For much of the nineteenth century, the issue of slavery divided and challenged Christians. The fact that it appears to us today as a straightforward moral issue allows us to see it with a clarity that often eluded Christians in the nineteenth century.

At the beginning of the nineteenth century the majority of Christians did not regard the issue of slavery as contentious. They were quite convinced that it was permissible and fully justifiable. Had they appreciated the difference between inherent and consequential ethical arguments, they might have contended as follows:

Slavery is inherently right. Men have clearly been created with differing capacities, some to serve and others to be served. This is evident both within nations and between them. So, within nations it is right that there should be differing social orders and it would be unnatural to attempt to overturn them. And between nations, some are created to serve and others to be served. It is natural for some nations to control, pacify and subordinate other nations. So, as it is Europeans who first 'discovered' other races and nations in the world it is they who should naturally be the served. Slavery is but a product of this: it is a part of the natural and created order.

Further, slavery seems to be condoned in the New Testament. Slaves are told, 'Slaves, obey your earthly masters with fear and trembling, single-mindedly, as serving Christ' (Eph. 6.5),

Philemon is not scolded for owning a slave, and hierarchical social relationships seem to be accepted without question (I Peter 2.18). Even the history of subsequent Christianity gives little indication that slavery, in itself, was considered to be morally wrong. There is no dichotomy apparent between attitudes in earliest Christianity and those in the post-Constantinian Church.

Slavery is also consequentially right. It produces enormous economic benefits to European and American society, allowing the growth of crops to feed and clothe a growing industrial society. Were it to be abandoned precipitately economic and social chaos would ensue and, perhaps, civil war (as, of course, proved to be the case in America). The natural and created social order might be destroyed and the released slaves would themselves be forced to live in urban squalor (as, indeed, they were).

To these ethical arguments might be added a set of guidelines on the morally correct ways of actually using slaves – a just-slavery theory:

On the assumption that the actual possession of slaves cannot be inherently wrong – it is morally neutral – there might still be 'just' and 'unjust' ways of using slaves. A notion of discrimination would suggest that slaves themselves should be treated properly. They should be fed adequately, treated humanely, provided with adequate accommodation, not be sexually abused, transported in viable conditions and given medical attention when ill. Further, the 'innocent' should not be taken as slaves, but only those belonging to 'races which were created to be slaves'. A notion of proportionality would suggest that slavery should only be used in proportion to need. It would be wrong to make ninety-nine per cent of humanity slaves to serve one per cent. Rather, as long as there is clear economic and social need for slaves, it is justifiable to use as many as would meet this need. Provided that all of these guidelines are kept, the use of slaves would appear to be morally justified.

Of course the two issues are not parallel in every respect, but it might seem that a rather better ethical case can be made out for the possession of slaves than for the possession of nuclear weapons. Slaves are actually mentioned in the New Testament, with clear advice about how they should be treated (Eph. 6.9), whereas obviously nuclear weapons are not. In retrospect, one can see that, even if not as apocalyptic as those now associated with nuclear weapons, some of the consequential fears about abolishing slavery were justified. And Christian tradition, up until the nineteenth century, was relatively consistent in legitimating slavery, showing distinctly less of the remorse that has characterized Christian attitudes towards warfare.

Fortunately, we now know that all of this is moral nonsense. Slavery still has not been fully abolished from the world, and it certainly cannot be disinvented, but most people now regard it as a moral abomination. For most of us the possession of slaves is morally wrong, the use of slavery morally unjustifiable and its abolition a moral necessity.

This remarkable change in attitudes and intentions was inspired initially by the deliberate social and political action of a single-minded group of Christians defying the accepted wisdom of both church and society. It was, perhaps, too optimistic of the authors of the report *The Church and the Bomb* to expect that the General Synod of the Church of England could endorse their specific commitment to unilateralism. In *Prophecy and Praxis* (Marshall, Morgan and Scott 1981) I argued, at length, that churches, as churches, tend to follow, rather than lead, public opinion on social issues. Until public opinion itself could generally favour unilateralism, it would seem unlikely that the General Synod could do so. Even the General Assembly of the Church of Scotland (which has a far more radical history) has found a commitment to unilateralism contentious and difficult to sustain. If it has been passed one year, it has tended to be modified or reversed the next. On the other hand, individual Christians, groups of like-minded Christians and sects (which I understood, in a sociological sense, to be religious bodies with exclusive membership and doctrinal boundaries),[36] *can* uphold positions on social issues which defy conventional wisdom. In other words, they are able, if they are so determined, to be prophetic in ways which are not usually open to churches. Such prophecy involves a risk of isolation, ridicule and even hatred. But, on the nuclear issue, I believe that more Christians should be prepared to take this risk. The very danger of the present situation requires action.

If churches, as churches, cannot usually be prophetic on social issues, they do have a crucial role in embedding general values into society.[37] Without endorsing the specific policies of particular governments, they have been able to embed a number of key values into British society during the course of this century. The Welfare State is not a specifically Christian product (although a number of strong Christians were involved in its creation), but it does seek to make concrete a number of values – care for the underprivileged, help for the stranger and compassion for the needy – which are central to the Gospel. The Christian roots of these values tend to be forgotten in a 'secular' society and regarded, instead, simply as common-sense values. Sadly, in some countries they are anything but common sense.

I believe that churches do still have this function of embedding values into society and that some of these values are highly relevant to the nuclear issue. In the previous chapter, I suggested that churches should be more prepared to display some of the paradoxical attitudes towards war apparent in the New Testament and in the history of the earliest church. These attitudes hold in tension both a strong concern about social stability and a revulsion at violence; both a compassion for a less than perfect world and the vision of a perfectionism possible within and beyond the world; both a concern for those who suffer and a preparedness to suffer oneself. Above all, in an age in which war and the possibility of war, is becoming more and more of a moral abomination, the churches should be becoming increasingly vociferous in their revulsion of modern warfare and of the weapons of modern warfare. In such an age, I believe that it is wholly wrong for churches to appear to be legitimators of these weapons or of the uses to which they might be put. If they cannot be specifically committed to unilateralism, they should at least be expressing unambiguous revulsion at the possession of weapons of genocide and urging politicians to find ways for their reduction and strict control.

Some groups of church leaders have recently been prepared to take the risk of specifying political options to effect such reduction and control. Notably, the US Roman Catholic Bishops in their *Pastoral Letter on War and Peace in the Nuclear Age* argue that it is important to specify actions as well as attitudes. But they are also well aware of the risks involved in doing this:

> We realize, and we want readers of this letter to recognize, that not all statements in this letter have the same moral authority. At times we state universally binding moral principles found in the teaching of the Church; at other times the pastoral letter makes specific applications, observations and recommendations which allow for diversity of opinion on the part of those who assess the factual data of situations differently (*The Challenge of Peace: God's Promise and Our Response,* CTS/SPCK, 1983, p. i).

None the less, they believe that their specific applications should be taken seriously. Amongst these, they recommend the following five ways of promoting peace in a nuclear world:

1. We support immediate, bilateral verifiable agreements to halt the testing, production and deployment of new nuclear weapons systems. This recommendation is not to be identified with any specific political initiative.

2. We support efforts to achieve deep cuts in the arsenals of both superpowers; efforts should concentrate first on systems which threaten the retaliatory forces of either major power.

3. We support early and successful conclusion of negotiations of a comprehensive test ban treaty.

4. We urge new efforts to prevent the spread of nuclear weapons in the world, and to control the conventional arms race, particularly the conventional arms trade.

5. We support, in an increasingly interdependent world, political and economic policies designed to protect human dignity and to promote the human rights of every person, especially the least among us. In this regard, we call for the

establishment of some form of global authority adequate to the needs of the international common good (*The Challenge of Peace,* pp. vf.).

Although still fairly general, some of these recommendations are contentious (e.g. whereas some argue for a strengthening of conventional forces in a non-nuclear world, the Bishops argue for a reduction of *both* nuclear and conventional weapons). None the less, I personally believe that they are right.

In the specifically British context, the BCC has risked even more detailed policy proposals. There are clear differences of opinion evident within the BCC and they admit that 'some of us consider that deterrence is inherently unstable and that if it should fail, the consequences would be catastrophic. Others are prepared to live with the doctrine of nuclear deterrence as a temporary – or possibly even long term – expedient, provided that governments are clearly determined to end and reverse the competitive spiral in nuclear arms' (*On Making Peace in a Nuclear World,* p. 3). Nevertheless, they make the following six policy proposals:

1. The Council considers that the United Kingdom, like France, is in a position to make a particular contribution to nuclear disarmament. Renunciation of independent nuclear weapons by Britain (and/or France) would add weight and credibility to arguments against horizontal proliferation. The Council therefore reaffirms its decisions of 1979 and 1980 and urges that the United Kingdom, while remaining within NATO, should progressively phase out British nuclear weapons, and in particular should not replace Polaris with Trident missiles.

2. The Council recalls its 1963 decision that the nuclear arms race constitutes 'an offence to God and a denial of His purpose for man'. The Council therefore urges that the United Kingdom should work within NATO for a deterrence and defence policy that becomes progressively less dependent on nuclear weapons.

3. The Council further recalls its 1963 decision that it is intolerable that there should be any question of the West using nuclear weapons first and notes that there is a growing world-wide consensus that the conditional intention to use nuclear

weapons first is offensive to Christian conscience. The Council urges that the United Kingdom should work within NATO for a no-first-use posture and policy, even if this should necessitate higher levels of conventional arms and forces.

4. The Council recognizes that governments seek to avoid moves that might destabilize the balance. The Council recalls its 1967 decision that Britain and France should be prepared to forgo the possession of nuclear weapons if this would promote non-proliferation, and does not consider that the progressive phasing out of British and French nuclear weapons would have a destabilizing effect. As long as Britain and France retain independent nuclear weapons, this Council considers that they should be counted in relevant East/West disarmament negotiations if this would make super-power agreement easier to achieve.

5. Acknowledging that a nuclear component in deterrence is likely to continue to govern relations between the alliances and that negotiations on nuclear disarmament are likely to be complex and lengthy, the Council considers that the deployment of new weapons on either side would not provide a sufficient reason for the breaking off of negotiations; the Council therefore urges that negotiations be pursued with vigour, even in the face of serious obstacles.

6. Considering the addition of further nuclear weapons on one side (even if to correct a perceived imbalance) will almost invariably provoke a similar build-up on the other (also to correct a perceived imbalance) this Council deplores the deployment of large numbers of Soviet SS-20 missiles and does not consider that the deployment of Cruise and Pershing II missiles in response will advance the cause of security and peace. In order to prevent further escalation and to halt the competitive spiral in nuclear arms, the Council calls for an agreed and verified nuclear freeze by the United States and the Soviet Union, thus precluding further development, testing, production and deployment of nuclear weapons by the two super-powers (*On Making Peace in a Nuclear World,* pp. 4f.).

Again, these detailed policy proposals will not be supported by all Christians or by all the member churches of the British Council of Churches. None the less, I believe that they are important. More specifically in relation to each, my own position is as follows:

1. I have questioned (through Beach) whether the British/French independent nuclear weapons have any serious deterrent function. I have suggested, instead, that they are more political than military weapons and that, as political weapons, they present a constant threat of, and temptation to, proliferation, as other nations also seek to become 'independent' nuclear powers. I believe that it *is* important that they are phased out.

2. I believe that current NATO policy is far too dependent upon nuclear weapons. The horizontal expansion of nuclear weapons has brought about the dangerous situation in which any serious confrontation between East and West may result in nuclear confrontation. Further, I have expressed doubts about whether even a 'limited nuclear war' can be contained and not escalate into an all-out nuclear war.

3. I believe that the NATO policy of 'first use' of nuclear weapons against an invasion of Warsaw Pact conventional forces is dangerous and unjustifiable. But, unlike the BCC, I have yet to be convinced that its renunciation should entail higher levels of conventional arms and forces, to provide an adequate defence system in Europe. Further, as human ingenuity devises ever more destructive conventional weapons, their moral justifiability should also be questioned.

4. Although I have argued that the British/French independent nuclear weapons should be phased out, I remain agnostic about whether this should be achieved through carefully phased unilateralism (in line with the Osgood guidelines and with the eventual goal of multilateral negotiation and weapons reduction) or through the urgent multilateral negotiation proposed by Beach. Despite the confidence of the BCC about what will or will not have a 'destabilizing effect', I believe that the current evidence is either ambiguous or lacking, and that great care is required. However, this does not excuse those in government from undertaking the task (particularly since, as I have suggested, the nuclear *status quo* is itself unstable). It is vital that the current high levels of nuclear

weapons should be reduced and the British/French independent nuclear weapons, lacking any clear military function, provide an obvious starting-point for this reduction. Further, I agree with the BCC and Beach that these British/French weapons should be counted in relevant East/West disarmament negotiations. The fact that they are not is bound to be a (justifiable) source of aggravation to the Soviet. To the latter it must matter little if the weapons that are pointing at them and that are threatening them with destruction, happen to belong to powers which are technically separate, but which in practice work together.

5. I believe that politicians should be urged to pursue multilateral negotiations on nuclear weapon reduction and strict control, with vigour, even in the face of serious obstacles. If politicians devoted as much energy to this task as they currently do to far more peripheral matters, it is difficult to believe that greater progress could not be made. It is not for a theologian to tell a politician how to negotiate, but it is proper for a theologian to stress that politicians have a moral duty to negotiate vigorously in order to make the world a safer place.

6. I believe that it is vital that the competitive spiral of nuclear escalation should be halted. Since the BCC Assembly of November 1983, the escalation that they feared as a result of the SS-20 and Cruise/Pershing II deployment has got worse. If the Cruise/Pershing II deployment was intended as a counter to SS-20 deployment, then the current deployment of SS-20 missiles in Eastern Europe and nuclear submarines off the West Coast of America are further counter-responses. With each move in this spiral, nuclear weapons expand and the world becomes more dangerous. It will not halt until one or other, or both, of the nuclear superpowers decides that there are already more than enough nuclear weapons in the possession of both to act as sufficient 'deterrents' (if that is indeed what they are).

Finally, I return to the theological themes of my introduction. Their belief in a God who created and redeemed this world leaves Christians with no room for complacency faced with the empirical facts about present-day nuclear weapons. All but the most bland experts admit that these weapons are expanding and proliferating and a significant number admit that they are also unstable and ambiguously concerned with deterrence. Whether we decide that the most effective way of reducing them is through carefully-planned unilateralism or through urgently negotiated multilateralism, they *must* be reduced unless we are to desolate this God-given world. At present they are *not* being reduced: they are being increased enormously. There must come a point at which even the most ardent deterrent theorist concedes that the world will not get safer with an ever-increasing amount of nuclear weapons available within it. Precisely because they believe that the world is 'given', Christians are required to respond to this gift with gratitude and acceptance, not with a preparedness to let this gift be destroyed.

Notes

1. To avoid unnecessary repetition, where I refer simply to a page number, without further explanation, the quotation comes from *The Cross and the Bomb.*

2. Delivered to, but not endorsed by, the General Synod of the Church of England in February 1983.

3. For full details of this destructive capacity, see *The Effects of Nuclear War,* Croom Helm 1980, by the Office of Technology Assessment, Congress of the United States, and the Report of the Secretary-General of the United Nations to the General Assembly, *General and Complete Disarmament,* 12 September 1980. A useful summary is contained in Roger Ruston, *Nuclear Deterrence – Right or Wrong?,* a study prepared for the Commission for International Justice and Peace of England and Wales, Catholic Information Service 1981. See also Samuel Glasstone and Philip J. Dolan (eds.), *The Effects of Nuclear Weapons,* US Department of Defense and Energy Research and Development Administration 3 1977 – itself usefully summarized in the Anglican Report, *The Church and the Bomb,* Hodder and Stoughton 1982.

4. See further, *The Military Balance,* London: International Institute of Strategic Studies 1982-3, p. 112.

5. Beach argues in a footnote at this point: 'SS-4 and SS-5 have enormous warheads (1MT) but are relatively inaccurate. From some points of view the much more discriminate SS-20 presents a less horrendous threat.'

6. See further, Gregory Treverton, 'Nuclear Weapons in Europe', *Adelphi Paper* 168, London: IISS 1981, p. 13.

7. Discussed fully in the Anglican Report, *The Church and the Bomb,* with useful tables as an appendix on 'Countries with Nuclear Facilities' and 'Major Nuclear Missiles of the First Five Nuclear Weapon States'. However, Beach finds some of the Report's discussion on this issue misleading (p. 131).

8. See further, Frank Barnaby in Günter Friedrichs and Adam Schaff (eds.), *Microelectronics and Society. A Report to the Club of Rome,* Pergamon Press 1982, pp. 245-52.

9. Niebuhr even argued that it would 'seem better to accept a frank dualism in morals than to attempt a harmony betweeen the two methods which threatens the effectiveness of both. Such a dualism would have two aspects. It would make a distinction between the moral judgments applied to the self and to others; and it would distinguish between what we expect of individuals and of groups' (*Moral Man and Immoral Society* (1932), SCM Press 1963, pp. 270f.). This sharp dualism is not without difficulties and Niebuhr tended to soften it somewhat in later life (see C. W. Kegley and R. W. Bretall [eds.], *Reinhold Niebuhr, His Political, Social and Religio. Thought,* 1960), but I shall argue in Chapter 5, that it is crucial to the issu. war.

10. Estimates vary – the Anglican Report, *The Church and the Bomb* (p. 157), suggests 150.

11. In *Prophecy and Praxis: The Social Function of the Churches,* Marshall, Morgan and Scott 1981, Chapter 6, I argue at length that theologians should become more aware of the possible social consequences of their ideas.

12. See further Frederick H. Russell, *The Just War in the Middle Ages,* Cambridge University Press 1975, and Joan D. Tooke, *The Just War in Aquinas and Grotius,* SPCK 1965. I compare Augustine and Aquinas (and Ramsey) at length in my *Textbook of Christian Ethics,* T. & T. Clark 1985.

13. Particularly in the General Synod debate of February 1983, see *Report of Proceedings,* Vol. 14, No. 1, CIO, pp. 237-306.

14. There are a number of good guides to the philosophical study of ethical approaches: e.g. R. M. Hare, *The Language of Morals,* Clarendon Press 1952; P. H. Nowell-Smith, *Ethics,* Penguin Books 1954; A. MacIntyre, *A Short History of Ethics,* Routledge & Kegan Paul 1967; G. J. Warnock, *Contemporary Moral Philosophy,* Macmillan 1966; Mary Warnock, *Ethics Since 1900,* Oxford University Press 1960; and Philippa Foot (ed.), *Theories of Ethics,* Oxford University Press 1967. A. V. Campbell's *Moral Dilemmas in Medicine,* Churchill Livingstone 1972, provides a clear, readable account of the three approaches outlined here and I discuss them in detail in my *Textbook of Christian Ethics.*

15. In recent Christian ethics, Joseph Fletcher's *Situation Ethics,* SCM Press 1966, is the most famous (and most criticized) attempt to defend this approach. However, there are strong reasons for questioning whether a wholly situational approach is relevant to social ethical issues such as those raised by nuclear weapons, since clear decisions *do* have to be taken in advance of situations. Paul Ramsey argued emphatically that 'no social morality ever was founded, or ever will be founded, upon a situational ethic' (*Deeds and Rules in Christian Ethics,* Scribners 1967, p. 20).

16. Roger Ruston has a useful discussion of other Roman Catholic ethicists who maintain that the possession of nuclear weapons is morally neutral. Instead, he insists that 'the possession of nuclear weapons is not like the possession of other weapons which may be used for good, bad or indifferent purposes. The reason for this is that it is not simple, physical, pre-moral possession we are dealing with: it is *preparation.* Nuclear weapons are always the hard core at the centre of a fully established, working structure of readiness to use when the conditions arise' (*Nuclear ~terrence – Right or Wrong?,* p. 61).

See further James D. G. Dunn, *Unity and Diversity in the New ~ment,* SCM Press 1977.

See further the still impressive 1924 Bampton Lectures of N. P. ~s, *The Ideas of the Fall and of Original Sin.*

~uther tended to distinguish sharply between what is fitting for a

Notes

Christian, as a Christian, and what is fitting more generally in society. In what is sometimes termed the notion of the two kingdoms, he argued: 'Christians do not fight and have no worldly rulers among them. Their government is a spiritual government, and, according to the Spirit, they are subjects of no one but Christ. Nevertheless, as far as body and property are concerned, they are subject to worldly rulers and owe them obedience. If worldly rulers call upon them to fight, then they ought to and must fight and be obedient, not as Christians, but as members of the state and obedient subjects . . . The office of the sword is in itself right and is a divine and useful ordinance . . . Suppose that a people would rise up today or tomorrow and depose their Lord or kill him . . . I have never known of a case in which this was a just action . . . we ought to suffer wrong, and if a prince or lord will not tolerate the gospel, then we ought to go into another realm' (*Whether Soldiers, Too, Can Be Saved*, in *Luther's Works*, Vol. 46, Fortress Press 1967).

20. *The Limits of Nuclear War* was written as a specific response to the American Secretary of Defense Robert McNamara's celebrated speech of June 1962, in which he argued that the 'principal military objectives, in the event of a nuclear war stemming from an attack on the Alliance, should be the destruction of the enemy's forces, not of his civilian population'. The slightly earlier *War and the Christian Conscience* was written (as is evident from the quotation from it) presupposing the MAD policy of the Dulles era.

21. The Anglican Report argues: 'This secret must be confined virtually to two or three top political leaders who, in a democratic society, might be replaced at any moment by others who did not share their views, and who could never be initiated into them in advance, because the matter could not be publicly debated' (*The Church and the Bomb*, op. cit. p. 153).

22. Frank Barnaby is doubtful of both the computers in control and of whether the politicians are really in control of the computers: 'We are being driven toward nuclear world war by the sheer momentum of military technology . . . we may not have the sort of intelligence required to set up the political and social institutions essential to controlling military technology' (*Microelectronics and Society*, p. 272).

23. However, Roger Ruston points out that Admiral of the Fleet Lord Hill-Norton, Lord Mountbatten, Lord Zuckerman and former Chief of Air Staff Sir Neil Cameron have all argued that 'in any battlefield use of nuclear weapons the risk of escalation must be immensely high' (*Nuclear Deterrence – Right or Wrong*, p. 35). It is an open question how far the military establishment itself favours the present high dependence on nuclear weapons.

24. The examples given in the final clause differ somewhat from one version of just-war theory to another. Ruston summarizes it as follows: 'The mode of conducting the war should be morally legitimate: (*a*) the innocent must not be killed by indiscriminate slaughter; (*b*) it must not

result in disproportionate evils to the enemy population, to the home population or to the international community' (op. cit., p. 15).

25. See further, my *Theology and Social Structure,* Mowbrays 1977, Chapter 2.

26. Bainton, *Christian Attitudes Toward War and Peace,* is a particularly useful historical survey. But see also Geoffrey Nuttall, *Christian Pacifism in History,* World Without War 1958; C. J. Cadoux, *The Early Christian Attitude To War,* London 1919; Peter Brock, *Pacifism in Europe to 1914,* Princeton University Press 1972; id., *Twentieth Century Pacifism,* Van Nostrand Reinhold 1970. Useful historical readers are: Arthur F. Holmes, *War and Christian Ethics,* Baker Book House 1975; Albert Marrin, *War and the Christian Conscience,* Regnery 1971.

27. See further, David Martin, *Pacifism,* Routledge and Kegan Paul 1965; J. Milton Yinger, *The Scientific Study of Religion,* Collier-Macmillan 1970.

28. See further Peter Brown, *Augustine of Hippo,* Faber 1967. Some of Augustine's changing political attitudes can be seen in the reader, ed. Henry Paolucci and Dino Bigongiari, *The Political Writings of St. Augustine,* Gateway 1962.

29. See Frederick H. Russell, *The Just War in the Middle Ages;* Joan D. Tooke, *The Just War in Aquinas and Grotius.*

30. See further my *Theology and Social Structure.*

31. See further Bryan Wilson, *Religious Sects,* Weidenfeld and Nicolson 1970.

32. There have been a number of studies of New Testament attitudes to war: C. J. Cadoux, *The Early Christian Attitude To War;* G. H. C. MacGregor, *The New Testament Basis of Pacifism,* James Clarke 1936; and Charles E. Raven, *The Theological Basis of Pacifism,* The Fellowship of Reconciliation 1952.

33. See further N. A. Simms, *Britain, Chemical Weapons and Disarmament,* Armament and Disarmament Information Unit, Sussex University, No. 2, Vol. 3, 1980.

34. Even the early Reinhold Niebuhr of *Moral Man and Immoral Society* insisted: 'No political realism which emphasizes the inevitability and necessity of a social struggle, can absolve individuals of the obligation to check their egoism, to comprehend the interests of others and thus to enlarge the areas of co-operation' (p. 275).

35. The full statement is contained in Roger Ruston's *Nuclear Deterrence – Right or Wrong?,* pp. 5f: see also the Pastoral Letter of US Roman Catholic Bishops, *The Challenge of Peace,* SPCK 1983.

36. For a full discussion of this sociological definition, taken from Max Weber's *A Sociology of Religion,* see my *Prophecy and Praxis,* Chapter 1.

37. Cf. John Habgood, *Church and Nation in a Secular Age,* Darton, Longman and Todd 1983.

Index